Is Catholicism A Cult?

Raymond Bauer

Scriptures quoted are taken from the KJV
King James Version, Cambridge, 1769.

Available on Kindle as an eBook from Amazon.com,
Amazon.co.uk and Amazon's other retail outlets and websites.

FOREWORD

I wish to record my sincere gratitude to Dr Bill Jackson (deceased) of Christian's Evangelising Catholics (Louisville, Kentucky, USA) for the insight he shared and instruction he gave over many years in the subjects of Roman Catholicism and the evangelisation of Roman Catholic people. I thank him especially for the very simple, yet so profound, truth that one does a job until it's done, when we're doing we're not done, when we're done we're not doing, we cannot be doing and done at the same time! This very clear principle sums up the difference between biblical Christianity and all false systems of religion. We are both wholly trusting Christ and saved (done), or we yet trust our works for our salvation (doing). My thanks also go to those experts who write upon such matters as the cults for making it necessary for me to write upon an issue that appears to be an enormous blind spot for them.

DEDICATION

In memory of Bill, a faithful servant of God.

TABLE OF CONTENTS

Contents

FOREWORD 3

DEDICATION 4

TABLE OF CONTENTS 5

INTRODUCTION 7

EXTRABIBLICAL REVELATION 13

A FALSE BASIS OF SALVATION 22

AN UNCERTAIN HOPE 28

PURGATORY 31

PRESUMPTUOUS MESSIANIC LEADERSHIP 47

DOCTRINAL AMBIGUITY 59

CLAIMS OF SPECIAL DISCOVERIES 75

DEFECTIVE CHRISTOLOGY 81

SEGMENTED BIBLICAL ATTENTION 101

ENSLAVING STRUCTURE 108

ONE TRUE CHURCH 113

FINANCIAL EXPLOITATION 125

DENUNCIATION OF OTHERS 130

SYNCRETISM 142

CONCLUSION.....................................153

THE NEED FOR RC EVANGELISM.................155

SOURCES 185

INTRODUCTION

There was a time when Catholicism, or Roman Catholicism, was clearly defined by Evangelicals as being a false religion. There was little or no equivocation in their stating this to be the case; they were not embarrassed to call a spade a spade, or to refer to the Pope as being the Antichrist. Today we think ourselves too refined for such straight talk. In days gone by, the days of the Reformers, the days of the Puritans, even right through to the early 20th century, there was ability among Christians to see error quite clearly and to name that error and its advocates even more clearly. Today we seem to be living in a time when Christians are unsure about just what is erroneous and that which is not. Confusion abounds within Evangelicalism; Protestantism is largely discredited, the very name having become a byword for bigotry. There are those who are seeking open union with Rome, speaking of that pernicious system of idolatry as if it were just another flavour of Christianity. The hymn writer wrote *"Our fathers knew thee Rome of old and evil is thy fame."* Yes, the old saints knew, but sadly the church today does not seem to have the same awareness, the same clear vision of that which is false. Why is this? Perhaps the Reformers were wrong, the Puritans were wrong, all the great church confessions were wrong and, if the modern ecumenist is correct, all the martyrs died needlessly? A short read of Foxe's Book of Martyrs or Van Braght's Martyr's Mirror will show the truth of the matter. As we examine Catholicism in the light of history we pose the question, somewhat rhetorically, can Roman Catholicism really be considered to be a cult, or are we merely seeking to invent brickbats to throw at a traditional target for Evangelical Protestants? Are we simply being unkind and further demonising an old and mistrusted enemy, or is there some justification for classifying the Roman Catholic religion with the cults?

Walter Martin is author of the book 'Kingdom of the Cults', a work considered by many to be the classic work on the cults. Mr Martin is considered to be an expert upon the subject, and yet, in the contents list of the book there is not a mention of Catholicism, nor is there a mention of Catholicism throughout the book. All the major cults are mentioned there, the Jehovah's Witnesses, the Mormons and the Moonies, but no Catholicism! I find it quite remarkable that Mr Martin does not include Catholicism with the cults for if he were to apply the same criteria to it as he does to those listed in the book Catholicism would not merely be included but would be top of the list. He writes: "From a theological viewpoint, the cults contain many deviations from historic Christianity. Yet, paradoxically, they continue to insist that they are entitled to be classified as Christians." (Page 11, Kingdom of the Cults). Is not this precisely the case with Catholicism! It is a sub-Christian cult masquerading as biblical Christianity.

This work is not intended to be a critique of Mr Martin, nor any other writer upon the cults. I think however that it is fair to say that anyone who stands where the Reformers stood, on the ramparts of biblical Christianity, as some of the experts claim to do, cannot fail to see the cult nature of Catholicism!

How do we know that any religious group is a cult? What are the criteria? What is it that marks Catholicism out as a cult? In order to answer these questions fairly we must use the same criteria for measuring Catholicism as we would for any other cult, and if the criteria fits then we must come to the appropriate conclusion. We cannot afford to be partial in this matter for our God in the Day of Judgement will have no partiality, He will reject all false religions and cults, regardless of how much they may appear to be Christian. A common excuse for not rejecting Catholicism is that they seem to have so much in common with orthodox Christianity. It is argued that Catholicism holds with the Trinity, the Creeds, belief in Jesus etc. However, anyone with a little understanding of what the Roman Catholic church officially teaches would know that their teachings are fatally flawed and do not stand up when examined in the light of Holy Scripture.

The Catholic christ, it will be seen, is not the Christ of the Bible; the Catholic trinity has *four* people in it. As for her attitude towards Holy Writ many of the cults have a more biblical view of the Scriptures. It will be clearly seen that Catholicism is indeed a cult. This will be proven using exactly the same yardstick as is used to gauge the measure of those groups generally accepted as 'The Cults', that yardstick being firstly, the Word of God, and secondly, the expert opinion of men such as Dr David Breese.

Dr Breese in his book 'Know the Marks of Cults' explains on page 16 "A cult is a religious perversion." It is a belief and practice in the world of religion, which calls for devotion to a religious view or leader centred in false doctrine. It is an organised heresy... When contrasted to biblical truth, a cult is seen to have distinguishing marks by which it can be labelled as being fatally sub-Christian." According to Dr Breese there are 12 distinguishing marks of a cult, they are:

Extra-biblical Revelation.
A False Basis of Salvation.
An Uncertain Hope.
Presumptuous Messianic Leadership.
Doctrinal Ambiguity.
Special Discoveries.

Defective Christology.
Segmented Biblical Attention.
Enslaving Organisational Structure.
Financial Exploitation.
Denunciation of Others.
Syncretism.

Some cults bear more of these marks than others do. Even true evangelical churches sometimes bear one or more of these marks in some degree, and this is to be regretted. However Catholicism it will be seen bears all twelve marks and to the fullest degree!

The cults are spiritual harlots and Catholicism is, as the book of Revelation and chapter 17 tells us, *"Mystery Babylon The Great, The Mother Of Harlots And Abominations Of The Earth".*

You will read within these pages of but a few of her abominable practices but even by these, and her relationship to other false religions, it will be seen that she who sits upon the seven hills of Rome, the one who is *"arrayed in purple and scarlet colour, and decked with gold and precious stones and pearls, having a golden cup in her hand* (and wooden men in her priesthood) *full of abominations and filthiness of her fornication."* This is she of whom it is written *"And I saw the woman drunken with the blood of the saints, and with the blood of the martyrs of Jesus."* Let us not make the mistake of thinking any less of Catholicism than that which historical biblical Protestantism has held her to be for Catholicism has not changed an iota of her filthy dogma, she has merely changed her dress to look less like the great spiritual harlot that she so clearly is.

EXTRABIBLICAL REVELATION

The apostle John in the book of Revelation, chapter 22, verse 18, writes *"I testify unto every man that heareth the words of the prophecy of this book, if any man shall add unto these things, God shall add unto him the plagues that are written in this book:"* A solemn warning against adding to the Word of God. It is the Bible alone that is considered to be the sole guide and rule of the true Christian's faith. To add to the words of the Bible is clearly forbidden but it is a common trait of the cults to add their own writings to those of the Bible, or instead of the Bible.

The so called Jehovah's Witnesses, more correctly labelled the 'Russellites', have their many books and pronouncements of their ruling council, the Seventh Day Adventists add the writings of Ellen G White, Christian Science adds those of Mary Baker Eddy, the Mormons add the book of Mormon, Doctrine and Covenants and the Pearl of Great Price. None of the cults seem complete without extra-biblical baggage and Catholicism is no different. A Christian could easily fit his or her 'rule of faith' into a pocket, but not the Catholic, it would require several large trucks to carry all that a Catholic is obliged to believe and obey.

Catholicism has an awful lot of extra-biblical revelation which she puts either on a level with Holy Scripture or above it. The prophet Isaiah wrote, *"If they speak not according to this Word, (Holy Scripture), there is no light in them."* There is no light in Catholicism, but there is a mountain of darkness which has been built up to hide the wonderful truths of God's Word from the eyes of poor deluded Roman Catholic people.

Dr Elliot in his extensive work 'Delineation of Catholicism' writes of the Roman 'Rule of Faith': *"The Scriptures are the rule and only rule of faith and practice. The Protestant rule is the Scripture. To the Scriptures the Roman Catholic adds, (1) The Apocrypha; (2) Traditions; (3) Acts and decisions of the church, embracing numerous volumes of the Pope's Bulls; ten folio volumes of decretals; thirty-one folio volumes of Acts of Councils; fifty-one folio volumes of the Acta Sanctorum, or the doings and saying of the Saints; (4) Add to these at least thirty-five volumes of the Greek and Latin Fathers, in which he says is to be found the 'unanimous consent of the Fathers'; (5) To all of these one hundred and thirty-five volumes folio add the chaos of unwritten traditions which have floated down to us since apostolic times. But we must not stop here; for the expositions of every Priest and Bishop must be added. The truth is such a rule is no rule unless an endless and contradictory mass of uncertainties could be a rule. No Catholic can soberly*

14

believe, much less learn, his own rule of faith." (Page 13, para 4). He certainly could not carry it to church with him, even if he were the world's strongest man! All of the extra-biblical writings of every cult put together would not amount to anything like the extra-biblical baggage of Catholicism.

Many extra biblical revelations within Catholicism are connected with the cult of Mary. A recently published book upon the subject, titled 'Meetings with Mary - Visions of the Blessed Mother' by Janice Connell speaks of Visionaries, Locutionists and Spiritual Directors. She tells us on page 17 that *"Messages obtained from apparitions, visions and locutions (voices in the head) are called private revelation..."* Most normal people would call seeing things such as these Catholics claim and hearing of voices in the head as lunacy!

She continues by writing *"Private revelations can come from external visions and apparitions such as those Saint Bernadette experienced at Lourdes, interior locutions such as Saint Joan of Arc heard, and interior visions or images such as Saint Thomas Aquinas saw."* I rather think that Rome had Joan of Arc right the first time around when they thought she was mad and burned her as a witch. (Not that I advocate the burning of mentally ill people.) *"There are many visions apparitions, and locutions, perhaps as many as all the people who have ever lived."* (Page 19). Here in these few sentences is a clear admission that Catholicism has buckets of extrabiblical revelations and what is interesting is that the author refers the reader to the apocryphal book of Tobit chapter 3 and the verses 16 - 17, an extrabiblical book, to support these errors. The author in other places seeks to lend weight to her case by referring to other apocryphal books. She also refers on occasion to church tradition, the Magisterium (the teaching authority of the church) and to church dogma. All of these are sources of extrabiblical revelation.

Below are some examples of extrabiblical 'Marian' revelations as collated by Dr Bill Jackson in his work 'The Vatican Bank'.

"The chastening comet draws near. Words of Jesus: `Houses will blow in the wind. Skin will dry up and blow off the bones. Many will die in the great flame of the Ball of Redemption."'

In the case of the above the name of the lady to whom the apparitions and through whom the voices come is Veronica Leuken, a middle-aged housewife. One of the unique communications is through photographs, with rays of light streaming on the statues, *"a supernatural scrawl - Jacinta 1972,"* photo of Exterminatus, the angel of death *"going forth to claim his own - all those who are not in a state of grace."*

Extrabiblical revelation through photographs – is that not weird? It is certainly nothing to do with biblical Christianity!

Another message that Veronica Leuken relayed from Mary concerns the Brown Scapular. Mary said, *"I cry tears endlessly when I know that every day My Son is confronted by numerous souls who have refused redemption that will come to them through wearing the Brown Scapular. If you wear My Scapular, you will be saved."*

A scapular is a religious garment worn under the clothing. It consists of two pieces of cloth a few inches square joined together by ties and is worn like a vest with one piece of cloth on the chest and the other on the back. According to Catholic legend in 1215 the *"Blessed Virgin Mary appeared to Simon Stock, General of the Carmelite order when it was in great trouble. She gave him a scapular which she bore in her hand, in order that by it "the holy [Carmelite] order might be known and protected from the evils which assailed it," and added, "This will be the privilege for you and for all Carmelites; no one dying in this scapular will suffer eternal burning."*

JOHN XXIII in the Sabbatine Bull claimed another vision. He said that *"the Virgin Mary appeared to him, and, speaking of the Carmelites and those associated to them by wearing the scapular, promised that, if any of them went to Purgatory, she herself would descend and free them on the Saturday following their death."* Clearly the best that a Papist could hope for would be to die on a Friday whilst wearing the scapular!

What falsehoods these people are peddling! The Word of God tells us that Jesus Christ is the only Saviour of men *"Neither is there salvation in any other for there is none other name under heaven given among men whereby we must be saved"* Acts 4:12.

"In 1973, in Akita, Japan, Our Blessed Lady came weeping with an announcement to a humble Japanese nun that God is about to punish the world with a punishment greater than the Deluge such as one will have never seen before. Mary said, *"Pray very much the prayers of the Rosary. I alone am able still to save you from the calamities which approach. Those who place their confidence in me will be saved.'"* I point the reader to Acts 4:12 again!

"From SIGNS OF THE TIMES, Sept-Nov '93, page 6. *"New Australian Visionary Receives Messages. An Australian woman who recently began receiving messages from Our Lord and Our Lady is helping to spark prayer and conversions "down under." The woman, known simply as "Josefina-Maria," began*

*receiving messages on September 20, 1990. Since then,
she has received over 1,000. As with other of today's
Visionaries, the Lord is using Josefina to warn the
world that the times of God's justice are at hand."*"

Here is but one individual that claims to have had more
than 1000 extrabiblical and contra-biblical revelations.
If she is typical of Catholic mystics then Janice
Connell's statement regarding the number of
apparitions could be close to the truth. If so, that should
worry all true Christians that so much heresy and
humbug is being put about. Connell's book is but
another collection of children's fairy stories and satanic
delusions.

I would not dare to say that God cannot speak today.
God is God. However I firmly believe that any
prophecies and words of knowledge must be weighed
and examined in the light of Holy Scripture. The Holy
Spirit will never contradict the Bible. There is a world
of difference between a person expounding a passage of
Holy Scripture to give its meaning and application and
setting something forth as though it were some new
thing from God when it clearly contradicts His written
word. We must always test the spirits therefore let this
impostor who purports to be Mary the mother of Jesus
keep silence in the Church of Jesus Christ! This is not
the voice of Mary but a deceiver.

Why should alleged Marian pronouncements, papal decrees and mumblings of the Magisterium be given any more credence than the writings of Joseph Smith the founder of the Mormon cult? Many Christians would see through the sheer nonsense that is the basis for the Mormon religion. They have no problem in discerning the truth that the tale of Moroni and the mystical plates is just that, a tale, adapted from an unpublished novel. However, these same Christians cannot seem to detect the fundamental flaws that exist in Catholic contra-biblical or extrabiblical revelations.

Joseph Smith's wacky tale is actually more believable than many Catholic claims for it begins with what suspiciously smacks of a plagiarised and paraphrased account of Revelation chapter one with his own imagination thrown in for good measure. Smith seems to have made an effort throughout his fairy tale to make it sound like portions of the Bible, which is more than can be said for some of the blatant nonsense that is found in Catholicism. This practice of making the false something like the genuine is a common trait in counterfeiting; in order to pass the phoney off as genuine it must have a semblance of the real thing. Catholicism also uses this tactic, but she is arrogant and thinks that Christians will swallow anything which bears a Christian label and so she makes little effort in many cases to disguise the fact that her extra and contra-biblical revelations, pronouncements and decrees are straight from the pit of Hell. Such blatant corruptions and perversion of the Divine Revelation of God cannot go unchecked, it is high time that Christians woke up and sounded the alarm concerning the cult nature of Catholicism and its extra/contra-biblical revelations.

A FALSE BASIS OF SALVATION

"The cults without exception obscure the truth and offer salvation on some other basis than that of a free gift that comes to us by grace of Jesus Christ." (Know the marks of Cults (DB) pg. 32).

Rome most certainly bears this second mark of a cult for it is here that perhaps Catholicism and Christianity are most at odds with each other. The teaching of Scripture is plain. Salvation comes to us by grace alone, through faith in Christ alone, *"Not of works lest any man should boast"*. *"Salvation is of the Lord."* It is not of works of righteousness which we have done, are doing, or hope to do at some point in the future, salvation is of Christ alone and that which he has done! *"For Christ is the end of the law for righteousness to everyone that believeth."* Romans 10:4. The Scripture is clear: *"Not by works of righteousness which we have done, but according to His mercy He saved us."* The biblical basis of salvation is that of 'grace', the unmerited, undeserved favour of God. The basis of the cults is that of works. Not of that which Christ has done, but what we must do.

One of the greatest selling points of the cults is that they give their followers religious things to do. This very much appeals to the flesh for man is a religious creature and so they perform their religious acts in the misguided notion that they can somehow aid their salvation! If it were possible that a person could be saved by works I would suggest that we all become Roman Catholics for it is the Roman cult that has the edge on all others when it comes to salvation by works.

Catholicism can give you literally thousands of things to do that are supposed to aid salvation. Catholicism is a system of works, a system outside of which, according to them, there can be no salvation! "What must I do to be saved?" asks the sinner. The Bible answers, *"Believe on the Lord Jesus Christ and thou shalt be saved!"* There is no equivocation here, no 'if', 'but' or maybe! How very different this is to the demands of the Roman cult, 'do this, do that, do the other, do, do, do, and do it often. Do a million and one religious duties and, just maybe, you will scrape through in the end! Quite the opposite of the biblical truth of *"Being justified freely by His grace through the redemption that is in Christ Jesus."* (Romans 3:24).

Catholicism is a man-made system of works whereby the 'faithful' hope to eventually attain Heaven having achieved righteousness through 'their' religious duties and observances. *"For they being ignorant of God's righteousness, and going about to establish their own righteousness, have not submitted themselves unto the righteousness of God."* (Romans 10:3). It is not by works of righteousness that we have done, but according to His mercy that He, Jesus Christ, has saved us, (those who are trusting in the merits of Christ alone for salvation). See Titus 3:5. By delving into Catholic publications it can be seen that Rome anathematises, (curses), those who teach salvation by grace alone! The St Peter's Catechism asks "Q135. Will faith alone save us?" The answer is supplied "Faith alone will not save us without good works." The basis of salvation within Catholicism is utterly false and alien to the teachings of Holy Scripture it is a sacramental system of works where the onus is upon man's religious deeds rather than reliance upon God and His Sovereign power to save!

Under the Catholic scheme of things Salvation is the goal, the prize as it were, and the means of attaining that goal, of winning that prize, depends upon human 'merit'. To be saved under Catholicism one must at the point of death have sufficient merit to warrant admittance to Heaven, if one does not have sufficient merit then a combination of merit earned by others and merit awarded because of sufferings in Purgatory must be acquired to gain entry. There is a little more to this but essentially this is the Roman basis of Salvation.

Merit is earned throughout life, primarily from each of the seven sacraments of the church. These are, Baptism, which they say is necessary for salvation, Confirmation, wherein the bishop is supposed to impart the Holy Spirit and the Mass which they say is offered to satisfy God for sins and to obtain grace. For grace read merit. Grace in the Catholic view is something tangible, a commodity to be bartered with between man and God. The sacrament of Penance "increases the Grace of God in the soul"! The remaining sacraments being, Anointing of the sick, otherwise known as the Last Rites, Holy Orders and Matrimony. Each of these affords those partaking of them favour with God.

The teaching of the Bible is diametrically opposite to that which Catholicism teaches. The Bible teaches that man is corrupt in all his faculties and because of his total inability to do ought for his own redemption God in His mercy has chosen a people to salvation for His own glory of His free and Sovereign choice without respect to our works so that all those for whom Christ died will come to Him and will be saved to the uttermost. This is a sure and certain salvation to all who will believe because every aspect of it is of God and not of man. This, in very simple terms, is what is known as the doctrines of Grace and when one takes time to compare this biblical teaching with that pernicious system of works called Catholicism one can see that the former is Christ exalting, God honouring biblical

Christianity, whilst the latter is utterly dependent upon the works of sinful men.

The sinner cries out "What must I do to be saved", "Look unto Me," says Christ "and thou shalt be saved". The cults answer:

"The material blood of Jesus was no more efficacious to cleanse from sin when it was shed upon the accursed tree than when it was flowing in his veins as he went daily about his Father's business." Christian Science.

"We affirm the moral responsibility of the individual, and that he makes his own happiness or unhappiness as he obeys nature's physical and spiritual laws. Man becomes a spirit after death, doing both evil and good, but he may be saved as he progresses from one spirit level to the next... Each must work out his own salvation." Spiritualism.

"An unnumbered crowd of faithful persons do not expect to go to heaven. They have been promised everlasting life on earth if they prove their faithfulness, by faith in Jehovah's baptism, provided they abide in him, keeping good conscience through faith and loyal service." Jehovah's Witnesses.

"The blood of Jesus Christ does not finally save anyone... Baptism is essential for salvation. You must

be baptised to become a true Christian." Armstrongism.

"Through the atonement of Christ, all mankind may be saved, by obedience to the laws and ordinances of the gospel." Mormonism.

"Be still and know that you are God." Eastern Mysticism.

"He (Jesus) must come again to consummate the mission he left undone 2000 years ago." Unification Church (Moonies).

In addition to the above we can include the false religions such as Buddhism, Islam, Hinduism and Judaism. All of these cults, sects or religions have a false basis of salvation and Catholicism has more in common with these than with biblical Christianity.

It can be seen that, as Dr Breese stated *"The cults without exception obscure the truth and offer salvation on some other basis than that of a free gift that comes to us by grace of Jesus Christ."*

AN UNCERTAIN HOPE

According to Catholic teaching, *"It is the sin of presumption to trust that we can be saved by God alone, without our own efforts"*! It is wrong, says the Catholic 'St Peter's Catechism' to believe the truth that Jesus Christ is able to save to the uttermost all that come unto God by Him! Catholicism calls the truth of God's infallible Word a lie and sells her people a false and very uncertain hope.

A friend of mine once asked a nun about her need for salvation, her response was, *"We will be saved, I hope"*. That's all the poor woman could say, 'I hope'. For her, and millions of others relying on the false system of Catholicism, they can have no assurance of salvation, assurance of sins forgiven and a place reserved in heaven for them. The cults rely on an 'uncertain hope' to be able to sell their people another supposed device to aid salvation. Within Catholicism these devices would be such things as sacraments and sacramentals, of which there are thousands, none of which can give assurance of salvation. Because salvation in the Roman system depends upon what we must do, and none can say how much must needs be performed, there can be no assurance of heaven as something that is presently attained, reserved, waiting for us.

We could never know whether we had done enough, hence a statement such as this from the alleged 'Holy Father': *"Death holds motives for apprehensive concern by the reason of the imminent judgement of God."* So said Pope Paul VI on the occasion of his 80th birthday. The one who supposedly had the keys of the Kingdom was frightened of death, he didn't know what awaited him, and he didn't know whether he would scrape through. If the supposed Vicar of Christ entered eternity with such uncertainty what assurance can the average catholic have?

The Bible tells us that the Holy Spirit, who is the Vicar of Christ, not 'Papa Roma', will guide us into all truth. If Pope Paul VI was the Vicar of Christ how is it he didn't know the biblical doctrine of eternal security, which Jesus Christ so clearly taught? *"I give unto them eternal life; and they shall never perish, neither shall any man pluck them out of my hand. My Father, which gave them me, is greater than all; and no man is able to pluck them out of my Father's hand."* John 10:28, 29.

The Pope died without hope! There is no hope in any Pope and no Pope can ever have any hope, for he is that Man of Sin, the Son of Perdition. It is a far better thing to be popeless than hopeless! Many dear souls have clung to that false and uncertain hope known as the doctrine of purgatory. This you will see is nothing but a wicked invention of an evil system designed to fleece the gullible from their worldly goods and any confidence in the salvation that is in Christ Jesus.

PURGATORY

According to Catholicism, *"Purgatory is a place where souls suffer for a time after death on account of their sins"* (Cat of Chris Doc). This doctrine has been an official teaching of the church since 1438 and grew out of the erroneous teaching that there are two tiers of sins, 'mortal' and 'venial', or big sins and little sins. Mortal sins, we are told, send you straight to Hell when you die and venial ones to Purgatory, where any number of Roman Catholic inventions can shorten the time spent there, all of which come at a price of course!

Purgatory has ever been one of Rome's greatest money-spinners through the sale of indulgences. An indulgence is an allowance, perhaps in the form of a certificate, which gives the recipient time off in purgatory for payment of a sum of money. Depending on the sins, which you might want to offload, the cost would be adjusted accordingly. In the days of Martin Luther the Pope's agent, John Tetzel, was promoting the sale of indulgences in order to raise funds for the completion of the building of St Peter's Basilica in Rome. Tetzel would arrive in a town or village with his entourage and set up stall in a prominent place and there he would sell these papal indulgences. He would tell the people *"At the very instant that the money rattles in the bottom of the chest, the soul (of your dead relative) escapes from Purgatory and flies liberated to Heaven".*

It wasn't only for the dead that one could purchase an indulgence, but for one's self, and not only for sins already committed, but also for sins which you intended to commit! A man could go and purchase an indulgence for adultery or murder, or some other wicked deed, and then go and commit that sin with the full sanction and blessing of the church. As the church was also the law he would get away with the crime scot-free!

Martin Luther saw through this wicked deception and as a consequence he prepared what are known as his 'ninety five theses' and nailed them to the church door, which was the normal place to publish a public notice. These theses were arguments, biblical arguments against the sale of indulgences, and it was Luther's stand against such abuses, and some other factors, that brought about the Reformation of the 16th Century. There is clearly a link between the sale of indulgences, which are still sold, or can be earned, today, and the Roman Catholic doctrine of Purgatory.

There is much made in ecumenical quarters of the fact that Roman Catholics are allowed to read the Bible nowadays, but what is little known is that they are only to believe what the priest tells them to believe it says! It may surprise you however that all Catholic priests are obliged to only interpret the scriptures in accordance with the 'unanimous consent of the Fathers'. This being the case begs the question, how on earth can they give an opinion on anything, when the only thing the Fathers agreed on, was to disagree about almost everything! There is one thing however that they did very much agree upon, and that was the refutation of any doctrine of Purgatory. Justin Martyr, Irenaeus, Origen, Chrysostom, Theodoret, Tertullian, Ambrose, Augustine, and others all denied the doctrine of Purgatory!

Many Roman Catholics today do not believe in Purgatory. It may surprise you however, I am sure, to find me saying that I do believe in purgatory. Before you think I've gone mad and that I am about to trot off down the road to Rome, let me explain what I mean by that:

All of us have been to purgatory! Everyone has, I hope, at some time in his or her life been to purgatory, indeed I would hope that each of us has been to purgatory today! I sometimes take my car to purgatory, people used to go to a public purgatory near their home, and I wish my children would spend a little more of their time in purgatory!

Purgatory is, if you haven't already guessed, *'a place of cleansing'*! If you were to place a sign on your bathroom door which reads 'PURGATORY', you would no doubt get some interesting comments from visitors, but it would be quite correct, for the bathroom is a place of cleansing. People sometimes use the phrase 'this is purgatory' when a task is difficult. Children whilst standing at the kitchen sink washing dishes might well think that is purgatory, and they would of course be right! Not because it is hard work, but because it is a place of cleansing.

All need cleansing: Men and women, boys and girls all need cleansing from time to time from the dirt and grime of this world, more importantly though, they need the cleansing from sin! All need cleansing from sin *"For all have sinned."* This includes both you and I, Kings and Queens, Popes, Pastors and Priests. *"All have sinned"*, *"There is none righteous, no not one"*. It is not the case that some have sinned, and some have not, *"All have sinned and come short of the glory of God"*!

From the moment of conception, every human being, with the exception of the Lord Jesus Christ, has a sinful nature: *"Behold I was shapen in iniquity and in sin did my mother conceive me"* (Ps 51:5). *"Wherefore as by one man (Adam) sin entered into the world and death by sin and so death passed upon all men"* (Rom 5:12).

All mankind has sinned against God and the Bible tells us: *"If we say that we have no sin, we deceive ourselves, and the truth is not in us. If we say that we have not sinned, we make Him (God) a liar and His word is not in us."* (1Jn 8ff).

The Bible clearly teaches the sinfulness of the human race, the total depravity of man: *"The heart is deceitful above all things and desperately wicked who can know it."* Man is at war with God, our sins have separated between our God and us, and we need cleansing from that sin that we might be reconciled to God.

Sin cannot enter Heaven: We cannot enter Heaven in the filthiness of our sins because we fall far short of God's righteous standards in our natural state. In order to enter the beauty of Heaven we must be purged of every taint of sin. A 99% cleansing in the bathroom might be alright, but a 100% cleansing from sin is required for Heaven: *"For there shall in no wise enter into it anything that defileth, neither whatsoever worketh abomination or maketh a lie".* (Rev 21:27).

Consider for a moment, the sinful state of this world with all of its horrors and atrocities: Murders, rape, muggings, perversions, thievery, sickness, pain, sorrow and death. All of this exists because of sin, *"The whole world lieth in wickedness"* (1Jn5:19), the sin of one man, Adam! The saying is that one bad apple makes the whole barrel rotten, this is also true of sin, and should any sin be allowed to enter heaven it would soon pollute the whole and in no time it would be as bad and corrupt as this present world!

God cannot allow sin to go unpunished; His justice demands it to be punished. God cannot allow sin to remain un-expiated; His holiness will not allow sin into His presence. Whoever we are, regardless of how morally upright and good we might think we are, we all need to be cleansed from the filthiness of our sin before we can enter into the presence of God and the purity of Heaven!

We cannot cleanse ourselves: So how can we obtain this much needed cleansing? We cannot cleanse ourselves! *"Who can say I have made my heart clean, I am pure from my sin?"* (Pr 20:9) asked King Solomon. Neither you, nor I says Jeremiah: *"Though thou wash thee with nitre (soda) and take thee much soap, yet thine iniquity is marked before me saith the Lord God"*. (Jer 2:2). Isaiah too is very definite about the filthiness of humanity and the inability to cleanse ourselves, listen to what he says: *"We are all an unclean thing, and all our righteousnesses are as filthy rags (menstrual cloths) and we do all fade as a leaf and our iniquities like the wind have taken us away."* (Is 64:6).

The Bible makes it plain that the very best we can do, the very best that we think to offer God, is not good enough and falls short of His righteous standard!

We need cleansing: *"Wash you, make you clean"* (Is 1:16) says the Lord for nothing that defiles shall enter Heaven. We cannot perform this cleansing ourselves. How shall we have this cleansing? We are altogether filthy, where shall we go for cleansing?

Purgatory is what we need: What we need is somewhere we can go to, prior to entering Heaven, where we can be cleansed. We need a purgatory! Well that's fortunate because the Roman Catholics happen to have one; perhaps that will do the job? Before we come to that, let us consider some other views of purgatory:

Pagan purgatory: In every religious system, except that of Biblical Christianity, if indeed it can be called a system, the doctrine of purgatory after death, and prayers for the dead, have always been found to occupy a place.

In Greece the doctrine was put forth by Plato who said: *"Some must proceed to a subterranean place of judgement where they shall sustain the punishment they have deserved"*.

In pagan Rome purgatory was also held up before men with no exemption from its pains. In Egypt, substantially the same doctrine was taught, and once introduced to the popular mind, and then the door was opened for all manner of priestly extortion.

Prayers or sacrifices for the dead are always hand in hand with purgatory. Of course prayers are, according to the religious but lost, always better when they are offered through a priest, but the priest isn't going to offer these without special pay!

Roman Catholic Purgatory is no different: This is precisely the case with Catholic priests today! There is a common saying in the Republic of Ireland, *"High money - High Mass, Low money - Low Mass, No money - No Mass"*. Ex-priest Joseph Zachello, in his book *"Secrets of Catholicism,"* poses the question: *"A rich man leaves $10,000 for Masses for the repose of his soul. A poor man leaves but $1. Who has the better chance of entering Heaven"?*

The Bible teaches us that the end of those who die in their sins is set, the decree of God is irreversible, *"Let him that is unjust, be unjust still, and let him that is filthy, be filthy still."* Again in Ps 49:6ff we read, *"They that trust in their wealth and boast in the multitude of their riches, none of them can by any means redeem his brother, nor give to God a ransom for him."* There are no second chances after death!

It may interest you to know, that according to Roman Catholic theology, both the rich man and the poor man have the same chance of making it out of purgatory, if such a place as the Catholics teach existed. For though the priest might be obliged to say 10,000 Masses for the rich man and only one Mass for the poor man, the priest, nor the Roman Catholic church have any say over where the merit of those Masses bought can be applied. That is God's prerogative. Only God can decide to whose account the merit of Masses is accredited to. He could give all the merits of the Masses Mr Murphy's family have bought to Mr Murphy's worst enemy. Of course neither family would know! Is not this a very uncertain hope?

The priest isn't going to tell his parishioners that the merit of the masses they have paid for might go to someone else. If he did that then they probably wouldn't invest in such a hit and miss 'hope' and of course because he wants to rake in as much money as he can, so he keeps quiet about the scam. The whole doctrine of purgatory has been adopted and adapted by the Catholic church in order to keep its people in fear and to wring their hard-earned money out of them.

This wicked doctrine teaches men and women that they can lead sinful lives with no worries because atonement can be made after death. The Roman Catholic, St Peter's Catechism states: *"All the souls in Purgatory will go to Heaven when they have atoned for their sins."* Note it says: *"When they have atoned"*! The Bible plainly states: *"It is appointed unto men once to die and after death the judgement."* JUDGEMENT! Not purgatory.

Perhaps we are being too harsh or have misunderstood the Roman Catholic position, so let us ask the local priest some questions about Purgatory:

[Excuse me sir, can you tell me about Purgatory as I hear that it is a place of cleansing and I really need cleansing from my sins?
Well what is it that you would like to know about it?
Could you first of all tell me where it is?
Well nobody is quite sure really. Some say that it is an actual place while others think it is but a state. Of those who do think it to be a literal place there are numerous shades of opinion as to where it is, but they are sure that it exists!
You mean even all the popes with their infallibility can't tell us where it is?
I'm afraid not, not one of them can say, but again, they are sure of its existence.

Supposing I was to somehow find my way there, perhaps stumble upon it, could you tell me how long I would need to stay there?

Ooh now that is a difficult one, to be sure, you see no one can be sure!

How about an educated guess?

I heard Father Murphy saying the other day how it takes about 30 - 60 years of praying and innumerable Masses to release Carmelite Nuns from purgatory.

They must be very sinful Nuns!

Oh no, not at all, Carmelites are a very holy order of Nuns.

If it takes so long to get these holy Nuns out of Purgatory, it doesn't look too good for the likes of me does it? Maybe it isn't as bad as some say it is, can you tell me just what it is like Father Murphy, what will happen to me there?

To be sure, we can't be too sure about that either, for you see the fact is that no pope has ever defined the sufferings of purgatory, but they do say that it is a place of cleansing fire. Indeed the Irish have a saying "O place of happy pains, and land of dear desires where love divine detains glad souls among sweet fires". Others have said that just one minute of Purgatory is worse than a thousand years of the worst torture.

Thank you Father Murphy but that sounds very painful, and rather uncertain, I think I'll look elsewhere!]

Perhaps the reader cannot imagine what purgatory is supposed to be like, so try this: When you have a moment to spare, put the hottest ring on your cooker full on. When it's glowing really hot then sit on it for as long as you possibly can, perhaps a week. If a week seems too long try a day, or a couple of hours. Remember, one minute of purgatory is worse than a thousand years of sitting on the burner of your cooker according to Roman Catholic teaching so a day on your cooker should be a cinch!

What absolute nonsense all of this is. If we were Roman Catholics, here we are about to make the most important journey of our life, and our death, and we don't know where we are going! We don't know how long we shall be there, and no one can tell us! To cap it all, no one has a clue what will happen to us there, though most agree it will be very painful! An uncertain hope.

This is the man made Purgatory of Catholicism. A wicked, despicable invention designed to rule people by fear and superstition. A cruel instrument whereby the priest is able to extract the last penny from the purse of the poor widow. A very uncertain means of attaining the cleansing which we all need lest we be eternally separated from the love and presence of our God! Praise Him that, *"We have a more sure word of prophecy."* 'What saith the scriptures?' should ever be our resolve, in all matters of faith and practice, not the vain philosophies of wicked men!

What does the Bible teach about Purgatory: Surprisingly, the Bible has a very clear teaching on the subject: *"Help us O' God of our Salvation for the glory of Thy name: and deliver us and PURGE away our sins, for thy name's sake".* (Ps 79:9) Asaph knew of the need for cleansing from sin, and what's more, he knew where the answer lay. In God, and not in any Roman invention of pagan antiquity.

The Lord our God knows of our need for cleansing, and He has provided such for us! God foretold of this provision through the mouth of the prophet Zechariah: *"In that day there shall be a fountain opened to the house of David and to the inhabitants of Jerusalem for sin and for uncleanness"* William Cowper wrote of this fountain in the wonderful hymn: *"There is a fountain filled with blood, drawn from Immanuel's veins, and sinners plunged beneath that flood lose all their guilty stains".*

This is the only Purgatory that there is! What wonderful news this is! The cross of Calvary is the only place of cleansing for sinners! It is here that the Lord Jesus Christ poured out His precious blood for sinners. *"The blood of Jesus Christ His (God's) Son, cleanseth from ALL sin."* Note that: *"All sin,"* not some, nor much, nor most - All sin! Christ has washed away all the sins of all of His people.

Just as God promises: *"Come now and let us reason together saith the Lord: though your sins be as scarlet, they shall be white as snow: though they be red like crimson they shall be as wool"*. This being the case then, quite clearly, there is no need for the secondary, and second rate, cleansing of the Catholic purgatory!

To say that there is anything to be added to the perfect work of Christ is to malign Him: *"For by ONE offering He hath PERFECTED them that are sanctified."* Those whom Jesus Christ has purchased with His own blood, those whom the Father has given Him, He has cleansed spotlessly by His one offering upon the cross. God tells us in His word: *"I am He that blotteth out thy transgressions, for mine own sake and will not remember thy sins." "As far as the East is from the West, so far hath He removed our transgressions from us."*

I want you to consider just how far God has removed the sins of His people: If God had said as far as the North is from the South, that would have meant that His cleansing was measurable, but God deliberately inspired David to write *"As far as the East is from the West"*. This distance is infinite, it cannot be measured. If you started walking East today and kept on facing the same way, you could walk East for the rest of your life. God has *infinitely* removed our sins!

Yes, I do believe in Purgatory! God's perfect purgatory, the soul cleansing blood poured out in the one offering of Christ upon Calvary. *"Blessed are the dead which die in the Lord, from henceforth: Yea saith the Spirit, that they may rest from their labours."* If the Lord Jesus Christ has effected purgation, and His blood cleanses from all sin, then there is clearly no need for cleansing after death! As we have seen in our examination of the Catholic idea of purgatory, cleansing after death is a very hit and miss prospect.

When men cease to trust the teachings of Catholicism, or any false hope, and begin to grasp wholeheartedly that which God has declared in His written revelation, the Holy Bible, then they will have assurance of Heaven, death will have no sting nor victory. For the Christian believer death has no power to give *"apprehensive concern"* for he, or she is resting in the one who saves from the guttermost, to the uttermost and at death is merely going home to their great love, Jesus! Catholicism's teaching is very different to that which the Bible teaches: *"These things have I written unto you that believe on the name of the Son of God; that ye may know that ye have eternal life."* (1 John 5:13). *"For our Gospel came not unto you in word only, but also in power, and in the Holy Ghost, and in much assurance."* (1Thess1:5).

There is indeed no hope in the Pope and his flawed system, only Jesus saves!

PRESUMPTUOUS MESSIANIC LEADERSHIP

"Only Jesus Christ deserves disciples," says Dave Breese, and how right he is. Jesus Christ alone is the perfect Son of God, the author and finisher of the true believers faith. He alone is our High Priest, Prophet, and King. He alone is our mediator, the only Head of the Church universal, both militant and triumphant. There is no hope in the Pope - only Jesus Saves!

Cult leaders are usually endowed with divine capabilities, or qualities, and the Bishop of Rome is no different. Both he and his followers make fantastic and blasphemous claims for him which are more numerous and more vile than the rest of the cults together. This however should come as no surprise for the Roman Antichrist is clearly pictured for us in 2 Thess 2:3-4 *"Let no man deceive you by any means: for that day shall not come, except there come a falling away first, and that man of sin be revealed, the son of perdition: Who opposeth and exalteth himself above all that is called God, or that is worshipped: so that he as God sitteth in the temple of God, shewing himself that he is God."*

Protestants have traditionally held these verses as speaking of the papacy and when one examines some of the clear facts about it one can clearly see why this view is held. The Roman cult insists that all must be subject unto the Pope or be damned forever, for he, they say, is *God on earth*! According to the Council of Trent of the 16th Century, whose teachings are still valid within Catholicism today, *"the Pope may dispense against the apostle, against the Old Testament, against the four Evangelists, against the law of God."* What the Pope says is to be believed above Holy Scripture and the Apostles.

He further claims to be no less than: *"Bishop of Rome, Vicar of Jesus Christ, Successor of the Prince of the Apostles, Supreme Pontiff of the Universal Church, Patriarch of the West, Primate of Italy, Archbishop and Metropolitan of the Roman Province, Sovereign of the State of the Vatican City, now gloriously reigning."*

The Roman Antichrist has made many abominable boasts throughout the centuries:

"To believe that our Lord God the Pope has not the power to decree as he is decreed is to be deemed heretical." John XXII.

"The Pope and God are the same so he has all power and authority." Cardinal Cusa.

"The appellation of God has been confirmed by Constantine on the <u>Pope who being God cannot be judged by man.</u>" Nicholas I.

Dr John Owen the great Puritan preacher said of the papacy: *"Never was there a more horrid deformed image made of so beautiful and glorious head* (Jesus). *All the craft of Satan, all the wits of man cannot invent anything more unlike Christ as the head of the Church, than this Pope is. A worse figure and representation of him cannot possibly be made...Some say "he is the head and husband of the Church", "the Vicar of Christ over the whole world"* (An Antidote to Popery).

Rome's own boasts prove Dr Owen's point: *"The Roman Pontiff, by reason of his office as Vicar of Christ namely, and as pastor of the entire Church, has full supreme and universal power over the whole Church, a power which he can always exercise unhindered."* (Vat II -Edited by Austin Flannery OP).

These evil men who boast that they are as God or that at the least purport to be his His visible representative on earth, are vile and disgusting creatures, not only in their office, but in their persons. Alexander Ratcliffe wrote *"To write of the Popes of Rome is to write of a body of sinful men, the majority of whom were barren of that true spirituality so essential in the servant of Almighty God. Rome's protagonists have gone so far as to compare the Popes to the mighty spiritual giants mentioned in the books of the Old and New Testaments, but instead of there being the least suspicion of comparison, there stand out a striking contrast which forces anyone who knows anything at all about the Popes and their Popery to conclude that, while the spiritual giants of the Bible were indeed men of God and servants of the Most High, the so-called Holy fathers of the Vatican have mostly been of their father, the Devil and the slaves, wittingly or unwittingly, of the Prince of Darkness, the author and leading light of that awful system known today as the Roman Catholic Church."*

Below are some further examples of just how wicked popes of Rome have been, and are:

"Between 882 and 984, eight popes were put to death by poison, strangulation or starvation. Between 896 and 903 there were no fewer than eight popes. John XII (955-963) when aged 19, was made pope by his father Pope Alberic. He turned the Lateran Palace into a brothel, and was murdered by an injured husband.

Benedict VIII (1012-1024) was originally one of the robber band of the Count of Tusculum. Benedict IX (1033-1045) was elected at the age of 12, and became a debauchee and a murderer. In 1038, there were three rival popes in Rome. In 1055, Leo IX raised his own papal army, but was defeated in battle and kept prisoner for 8 months. Gregory VII (1073-1086), was one of the most capable popes, but was as arrogantly power-drunk as was Hitler; and lived to see Rome sacked by the Normans and Saracens, and died in exile. He declared that " He alone held the keys to Heaven and Hell ; and the power to give (or take away) Empires, Kingdoms, Duchies and the position of all men."

Innocent Ill (1199-1216) annulled our progressive Magna Charta, but his action was treated with disdain by the English. Innocent IV legalised Torture in 1252, although it never was introduced into England, Denmark, Castile or Scandinavia whose kings objected to it. Boniface IX (1392) was one of the most unscrupulous extortionists in an age when papal extortion had become a fine art. Dispensations, Indulgences and Exemptions all had their price, and his Italian wars required a bottomless purse. Innocent VII (1404-1406) had a very brief reign during which the Vatican was sacked and he fled- in terror. Alexander V (1409-1410) never entered Rome owing to the disturbed state of Italy.

John XXIII (1410-1415) started life as a pirate, and was eventually deposed for unsuitability. His loss did not matter very much, as there were two other elected popes at the time. Calixtus III (1455-1458) promoted two of his 20-year-old nephews to be cardinals, and a third was made Prefect of Rome. Innocent VIII (1484-1493) had a very large family, and ennobled many of his children, expenses being paid for out of Church monies. Alexander VI (1493-1503) was a Borgia, and, under him the Papacy sank to its lowest depths of degradation. He was the father of the notorious Caesar and Lucretia Borgia. But his wars and sins did have a certain merit, as they revealed to the European people the utterly irreligious scandals to which the Vicars of Christ had fallen. His criminal misbehaviour contributed towards the success of the Reformation. Leo X (1513-1522) was made a cardinal at 14. In his youth he possessed-with their revenues the canonries of six chapters, six rectories and sixteen abbeys.

In 1570 Pope Pius V excommunicated and 'dethroned' Queen Elizabeth 1. The papal Bull described her as being "the pretended queen of England, and steeped in vice."

It would be interesting if we could possess a record of the remarks which the very capable Tudor monarch must have made on receiving that piece of papal impertinence. Some Mediaeval popes reduced every spiritual office to a fixed price. John XXIII even insisted on a system of 'payment before institution' to avoid tiresome wrangling. To pay for bishoprics, etc., money which was not forthcoming on a 'cash down' basis could be borrowed at exorbitant rates from the financial department of the Vatican.

Sexual immorality was widespread. When, in 1414 John XXIII and a vast retinue of bishops and minor clerics attended a Church Council at Constance, no fewer than 1,500 prostitutes descended upon the city. It should not be imagined however that it is only the early or medieval popes who have transgressed against Civilisation. Pius IX (1846-1878) and Pius XI (1922-1939) are two modern popes with really dreadful records.

PIUS IX was the pontiff who devised and introduced the dubious 'Infallibility' theory-not without considerable opposition from his colleagues. He hated Social Reform. During his reign the peoples of Europe were emerging from a period of Tyranny under the kindly spirit of Liberalism. His opposition to this sort of Progress made him so unpopular that in 1848 he had to flee secretly from Rome in disguise. This Holy Father had to stay away from Rome for two years until things had cooled down. So intensely unpopular was he with the Romans that, when his body was taken for final burial, the Vatican thought it would be wiser to have it moved by night. Even so, it was discovered, and there were ugly demonstrations by enraged citizens who threw mud at the hearse.

PIUS XI (1922 to 1939) was a man who similarly was contemptuous of democratic or liberal ideas. His policy was one of hostility towards progressive trends in modem social problems. He supported Hitler and Mussolini in their early days, hoping that (with their assistance) he could extend the influence of the Roman Catholic Church in world affairs. In doing so he unwittingly paved the way for World War Two, by lending his vast influence to encourage Fascism and Nazism in their early difficult days. Any man who had a part in fostering such regimes of horror has to stand before the bar of history with an unenviable conscience. Pius XI holds very considerable responsibility for the havoc which the " dogs of war " committed between 1939 and 1945." (Freedom's Foe - A Pigott)

Such are some of the men who have purported to be the Vicar of Christ! Others are as bad, if not worse.

At the Lateran Council of 1512 Pope Leo X was described as follows: *"The Lion of the Tribe of Judah, King David, the Saviour who was to come, King of Kings and monarch of the world, holding two swords, the spiritual and the temporal, in whom should be fulfilled the prophecy "all kings shall fall down before him," to whom alone all power was given in heaven and in earth. "*

Dr Loraine Boettner in his classic work on this wicked cult of Catholicism, 'Roman Catholicism' writes of the worldly character of the papacy:

"Christ does not need such a deputy as Rome claims that she has in the pope, and history shows that all men who have attempted to function in that capacity have failed miserably. Over against the claims of Rome the Reformers set the Word of God. Against Rome's "Thus saith the church," they placed a "Thus saith the Lord." Luther and Calvin were willing to recognise only Christ as the Head of the Church and denounced the pope as the Antichrist. Indeed, the claims of the pope to universal and total authority over the souls of men and over the church and nations are such that either he is all that he claims to be-the vicar of Christ and the vice-regent of God or he is the biggest impostor and fraud that the world has ever seen!

The fallacy of the claim that the pope is the vice-regent of Christ is apparent in the glaring contrast between him and Christ. The pope wears, as a fitting symbol of the authority claimed by him, a jewel-laden, extremely expensive crown, while Christ had no earthly crown at all-except a crown of thorns which He wore in our behalf. In solemn ceremonies the pope is carried in a portable chair on the shoulders of twelve men, while Christ walked wherever He needed to go. We cannot imagine Christ, who came not to be ministered unto but to minister, being carried in luxury on the shoulders of men. The pope is adored with genuflections (a bowing of the knee in reverence), he is preceded by the papal cross and by two large fans of peacock feathers, and his garments are very elaborate and costly, all of which is out of harmony with the person and manner of Christ. The pope lives in luxury with many servants in a huge palace in Vatican City, while Christ when on earth 'had not where to lay His head." Many of the popes, particularly during the Middle Ages, were grossly immoral, while Christ was perfect in holiness.

Christ said that His kingdom was not of this world, and He refused to exercise temporal authority. But the pope is a temporal ruler, just like a little king, with his own country, his own system of courts, vassals, coinage, postal service, and a Swiss military guard (100 men in sixteenth century uniforms) which serves as a papal bodyguard. The popes claim political power, and for many years ruled the Papal States, which stretched all the way across Italy and contained 16,000 square miles and a population of approximately 3,000,000. Those states were confiscated by Italy, under the leadership of the patriot Garibaldi, in 1870, and since that time the popes have been limited to Vatican City, located within the city of Rome, which has an area of about one-sixth of a square mile and a permanent population of about 1,000, with some 2,000 more employed there. In maintaining his claim to political power the pope sends ambassadors and ministers to foreign governments, and in turn receives ambassadors and ministers from those governments. As of October 12, 1960, 31 nations maintained ambassadors at the Vatican and received ambassadors from the Vatican, and 11 nations maintained ministers there. In each country to which a papal ambassador is sent Rome seeks to have her ambassador designated as the dean of the diplomatic corps, thus giving him rank above the other ambassadors. The affairs of the Roman Church are controlled by a bureaucracy that is tightly controlled, completely authoritarian, and self-perpetuating, all of which is in striking contrast with the New Testament principles of church government in which the affairs of the church were in the hands of the people. The pope is elected by the cardinals, who then disband and have no further power to censure any of his actions. New cardinals are appointed by the pope, without necessary consultation with anyone; nor is there any limit on the number of new cardinals that he may appoint, the full number of the college of cardinals having remained at 70 for centuries until recently when pope John XXIII increased the number to 85.' The bishops too are appointed by the pope, and may be promoted, moved, demoted, or dismissed as he pleases. The priests and nuns are chosen by the bishops, and are promoted, demoted, or transferred by them, without explanation if they so choose. And the people must be obedient to the priests, although in all of that elaborate system they have no official voice at all, nor is there any official channel through which they can express their ideas or preferences in church affairs. The papacy, therefore, is not a spiritual unity in Christ, but an external unity under the pope, a cloak which covers divisions and dissension between the various church orders which on occasions have emerged with much rivalry and bitterness."

The arrogance of the Roman Papacy knows no bounds, there are many other blasphemous claims made by Catholicism for its leader, but here is sufficient to demonstrate that Catholicism bears the cult mark of Presumptuous Messianic Leadership!

DOCTRINAL AMBIGUITY

To see a clear example of such within Catholicism one need only to consider the strange beast known as the Evangelical Catholic Movement. This group epitomises the Jesuitical double talk that is common throughout Catholicism; semantics is the name of the game. The Jesuits are the shock troops of the Vatican, and through the years they have been kicked out of every country they have polluted with their vile presence. They have ever been two-faced, it is part of their creed to lie and deceive in order to achieve their ends, and indeed the very word Jesuitry is in common usage in the English language to denote a less than honest attitude. The Readers Digest Oxford Wordfinder describes Jesuitical as *"dissembling or equivocating, in the manner once associated with the Jesuits."*

Edmond Paris in his book 'The Secret History of the Jesuits' gives clear examples of Roman ambiguity: Page 64 *"The Divine Law prescribes: "You shall not bear false witness." "There is false witness only if the one who took the oath uses words which he knows will deceive the Judge. The use of ambiguous terms is therefore allowed."* Catholicism often makes doctrinally ambiguous statements such as those contained in their leaflet *"What is an Evangelical Catholic"*, where Jesuitical ambiguous language is used very deftly to convince Christians that there is such a thing as an 'Evangelical Catholic'. This of course is an impossibility, a clear contradiction in terms; this is tantamount to saying one is a 'Protestant Catholic', sheer nonsense!

Dave Breese writes on page 61 of his book *"One of the most mentally frustrating experiences in life is to attempt to decide exactly what a religious promoter meant by what he said."* This is certainly true of Catholicism, therefore it may be useful here to define some Evangelical terminology for which Catholics have another meaning, whilst using the same terms, (otherwise known as Jesuitry!). Let us examine the strange beast known as Evangelical Catholics.

There are those within the catholic church who would describe themselves as being Christian Catholics or Evangelical Catholics. I intend to show you why I believe that the phrase *'Evangelical Catholic'*, and you can take with that the phrase *'Catholic Christian'*, is a misnomer, a falsehood, an impossibility. One is either an Evangelical or a Catholic, one is either a Christian or a Catholic, and you cannot be both at the same time! To attempt to do so is a clear case of 'doctrinal ambiguity'. I hope to demonstrate this as we proceed!

I first heard of *'Evangelical Catholics'* somewhere around the beginning of 1991 whilst involved with the work of *'Christians Evangelising Catholics'* when I received a leaflet in the post entitled *'What is an Evangelical Catholic?'* The person who sent it to me was a Charismatic Catholic and in his letter he said something to the effect of:

'Look I have read your literature and you have got it all wrong, we Catholics believe much the same things as you Protestants do these days. At least that which is in this leaflet is what I believe'.

I read through the leaflet and found it very exciting, and here is why: On turning to page 2 of the leaflet I read the following: *"Evangelical Catholics would affirm:*

That salvation cannot be earned, it is a free gift - however, the evidence of good deeds that one has become a committed Christian must then follow.

That there is only one mediator between God and men, the person of Jesus Christ (1 Tim. 2:5).

The priesthood of all true believers which is that a committed Christian has direct access to the Father through Jesus.

That Scripture in its entirety (both Old and New Testaments) is the inspired authoritative Word of God.

That the Eucharist (or Mass) is not a repetition of Calvary, i.e., Jesus died once and for all. The priest and people enter into that one all sufficient sacrifice by Grace.

The eternal reality of Heaven and Hell - Heaven for those who are redeemed and hell for those who are wicked."

All wonderful stuff there! One might perhaps in the light of such startling revelation decide that we need not to evangelise Roman Catholics after all, that we should concentrate our efforts elsewhere. There are many who have swallowed that lie and have done just that, they have abandoned the historical view of Catholicism, believing it to have moved its doctrinal position, and have signed up to the document *'Evangelicals and Catholics Together'* wherein they have agreed not to evangelise Roman Catholics.

So are these the teachings of Rome today, is this what Roman Catholics believe or is the 'Evangelical Catholic' movement just a group of radicals within Catholicism who are cocking a snook at Mother Church. There are those within Catholicism who seem to delight in not towing the official line, perhaps this group are such? Whilst this is plausible it is simply just not the case for this document is *printed with ecclesiastical permission,* it has the official sanction of the Roman Catholic Church and is consequently an official publication of the Roman Catholic church. Indeed there is a note on page 3 of this document which states that the *"points above are part of the official teaching of the Roman Catholic church."*

So have we got it all wrong? Has Rome shifted its doctrinal position into line with Evangelical Christianity? They do seem quite open with their statement that *"The Roman Catholic church is a Christian church that has taken on some un-Christian practices over the centuries."* Perhaps we judge them too harshly, maybe they have changed!

Their statement goes on to say *"However a major renewal of the Holy Spirit has and is taking place directly as a result of the Second Vatican Council addressing these issues."*

According to this statement *Vatican II* is where it all changed, *this is where the issues where addressed!* So what conclusions did Vatican II come to concerning these matters? Let us examine each of the statements found in their tract and weigh the evidence, let us compare them with official Roman Catholic teaching. I would just like to point out at this time that it matters not whether I refer to pre-Vatican II writings, or not, as each Bishop in attendance swore to abide by all that previous councils had declared, and in particular the Council of Trent! Trent still stands today as valid as ever in the Roman Catholic church!

Statement 1: *"Evangelical Catholics would affirm: That salvation cannot be earned, it is a free gift - however, the evidence of good deeds that one has become a committed Christian must then follow."*

What wonderful truths these are, how very evangelical! Is this really what the Roman Catholic church teaches today? In his post Vatican II book, *'The Teachings of the Catholic Church'*, Karl Rahner, an eminent Roman Catholic theologian sets forth the answer to many of the questions which we might have about this issue.

In contradiction to the statement we are considering we find that the Council of Trent, sixth session, 1547, Decree on Justification states: *"Canon 746: If anyone* *shall say that the sinner is justified by faith alone, meaning that nothing else is required to co-operate in order to obtain the grace of justification, and that it is not in any way necessary that he be prepared and disposed by the action of his own will - <u>Anathema Sit</u>"!*

For believing what the so-called Evangelical Catholics say that they believe, and that which we Protestants most assuredly do believe, *"That salvation cannot be earned, it is a free gift"*, both they and we are cursed by Rome! Here are two totally opposite statements, both of which claim to be the official teaching of Rome, both cannot be right so which one is the official line?

St Peter's Catechism says: *"It is the sin of presumption to believe that we can be saved by God alone without our own efforts."* This is the true position of Rome and it is reinforced by statements such as this one by Bishop Fulton Sheen *"Reconciliation is thy work, atonement is mine."* Either the authors of the tract are very confused or they like to play the well-known Jesuit game of semantics! Surely they wouldn't be lying!

Statement 2: *"There is only one mediator between God and men, the person of Jesus Christ."*

Again what a glorious truth this statement is and what great joy and rejoicing there would be among the people of God if this was truly what Roman Catholics believed. Sadly the official position is quite contrary for not only does every priest claim to be a mediator through the office of the confessional but we also see Mary elevated to the status of Mediatrix.

Perhaps I am exaggerating the position of Mary within Catholicism! Let us see:

Pope Leo XIII's encyclical - FIDENTUM (1896) speaks of Mary's mediatory role: *"No-one can think of anyone who has or ever will contribute so much to reconciling man to God as she (Mary) has done and does."*

Prior to this statement this same Pope in another official letter, OCTOBRI MENSE (1891), had this to say: *"Nothing comes to us except by God's will, through Mary; so that, just as no-one can attain to the supreme Father except through the Son, to a certain extent, no-one can attain to the Son except through the mother."*

This is really a very devious statement that we have here. Yes they can say that Christ is the only mediator between God and men, (not-with-standing the priests in the confessional and of course the blasphemous title of Supreme Pontiff, given to the Popes), because they say that no one can come to Jesus except through Mary! Semantic, ambiguous and Jesuitical language again!

Statement 3: *"Evangelical Catholics...Would affirm the priesthood of all true believers."*

Would they really? I find this very hard to swallow in view of their priestcraft. A practice which is clearly condemned in Holy Scripture (cf. Rev 2:6:). The whole concept of a priestly caste and subjugated laity is the essence of Catholicism. A mysterious priesthood, performing mystical rites on behalf of a bewildered, and often superstitious people.

Pope Pius XII's encyclical, MEDIATOR DEI, of 1947 commences: *"The fact that the faithful take part in the eucharistic sacrifice does not mean that they also possess the power of the priesthood"* It continues to say: *"There are some who, holding a view not far from errors that have already been condemned, teach that the New Testament knows of no priesthood other than that which is common to all the baptised...It is not necessary to show how plainly these captious errors contradict the truths we asserted above in speaking of the special position that the priest holds in the mystical body of Christ."*

If we take this statement as it is, without any particular spin on it we must conclude that, for a Roman Catholic to assert that they hold to the evangelical doctrine of the priesthood of all believers, they must condemn themselves out of their own mouths for it is contrary to the official teaching of the Roman Catholic Church. However, once more they are playing semantics here for there is within Roman Catholic thinking a sense in which those attending Mass are said to be exercising a common priesthood. What is certainly not meant is the evangelical belief of the priesthood of all believers!

Statement 4. *"Scripture in its entirety (both Old and New Testaments) is the inspired authoritative Word of God."*

Notice here the importance of the word *'entirety'*. Though on the face of it this sounds like a clear evangelical statement, it is in fact, yet again, a very deceptive statement, for in reality this, in their way of thinking, would include the Apocrypha. To Rome the entirety of Scripture includes those books of doubtful origin which the Christian Church rejected long ago! A true sounding statement by them, but they have clearly been very economic with it and ambiguity is evident once more!

Statement 5. *"The Mass is not a repetition of Calvary."*

Now what is wrong with that statement? Surely we can't find fault with that! You might be thinking. This is what evangelicals have always said! That may well be the case but it is not what Rome has taught for she has always asserted that the Mass is not a repetition of Calvary, but a continuation of it!

We should also be careful not to swallow the lie that the Mass is merely a memorial or thanksgiving. According to Roman Catholic teaching the Mass is most certainly a *Propitiatory sacrifice for the living and the dead*! St Peter's Catechism again clears up the matter:

"Is the Blessed Eucharist a Sacrament only? The Blessed Eucharist is not a Sacrament only: it is also a sacrifice". "Is the Holy Mass one and the same sacrifice with that of the cross? The Holy Mass is one and the same sacrifice with that of the cross."

Yes it is true that the Mass is not a repetition of Calvary, nor is it a continuation. Our blessed Lord Jesus Christ has Himself clearly declared upon the cross *"It is finished"*. And yet *every priest standeth daily ministering, offering oftentimes the same sacrifices which can never take way sins, but this man, Christ*

69

Jesus, after He had offered one sacrifice for sins, forever, sat down!

Statement 6. *"The eternal reality of Heaven and hell - Heaven for those who are redeemed and hell for those who are wicked."*

Taken at face value this statement is fine, however as everything else in their document has been very ambiguous to say the least, I do suspect that they would like to give the impression that they no longer hold to the doctrine of a secondary place of cleansing such as purgatory. This is not the case for Purgatory is still very much Roman Catholic official teaching.

In all of the points that we have considered thus far I am convinced that there has been a deliberate effort on the part of those who constructed this document to deceive its readers. I am convinced that the authors have deliberately sought to confuse both those Roman Catholics who are genuinely searching for the truth, and those within evangelical churches who are not as discerning as they perhaps need to be.

If this document is a huge deception, what is the intended goal of it all? Tom Forrest, the priest running the Charismatic Catholic Evangelisation 2000 initiative for the Vatican gave the game away at *'Indianapolis*

90' when he made the following announcement to the thousands gathered there:

"Now because I love being a Catholic, my job, my role in evangelism is not just to make Christians. Our job is to make people as richly and fully Christian as we can by bringing them into the Catholic Church. No, you don't invite someone to become a Christian; you invite them to become Catholics. There are seven Sacraments and the Catholic Church has all seven. On our altars we have the body of Christ; we drink the blood of Christ. As Catholics we have Mary, and that Mom of ours, Queen of Paradise, is praying for us till she sees us in glory. As Catholics - now I love this one - we have Purgatory. Thank God! I'm one of those people who would never get to the Beatific vision without it! It's the only way to go. Our job is to use this remaining decade evangelising everyone we can into the Catholic Church."

The purpose of the Evangelical Catholic movement, and this document which we have been examining, is quite simply to bring people into the Roman Catholic church under the guise of Evangelical Christianity. It is an ecumenical Trojan Horse.

So what is an Evangelical Catholic? Is it what the document we have been considering says one is? I suggest that those who say they are Evangelical Catholics are either:

Confused Christians: There may be a number of individuals who would say that this tract is what they believe but for one reason or another God has not yet led them out of the Catholic system. Perhaps they have been truly born again but have been bamboozled by such Jesuitry as this.

Confused Catholics: People who are sincere enough but have not been born again, people who are perhaps still searching.

Deliberate deceivers: Such as I believe are they who put together this document and others like it. I suggest that this document was written with the deliberate aim to deceive all kinds of people, on both sides of the fence. There are but two sides for one is either an Evangelical, or a Catholic, one cannot be both at the same time! An Evangelical is one who is trusting in the finished work of Christ. Evangelicals would affirm that they have no priest but Christ, no sacrifice but Calvary, no confessional but the Throne of Grace and no authority but the Word of God!

As we have said elsewhere in these pages, a Roman Catholic is one who is trusting in the Roman Catholic system of religion for their salvation and perhaps doing their best to attain Heaven at last via the sacraments and purgatorial fires and many other unbiblical means. Catholicism tells the sinner, *'DO'*, whilst Christ says *'Done'* Christianity is a *'Know-so'* salvation, whilst Catholicism is but a *'hope-so'* salvation.

Perhaps my remarks about this matter could be construed as being unloving by some. Is it right for one to be so suspicious of what may after all be the genuine belief of a Catholic? Such as that of the friend who originally passed on the document. Though my friend did not realise it at the time, the moment he stopped trusting in what he was doing and what his church required of him, as soon as he trusted in the finished work of Christ, he had ceased to be a Roman Catholic and had become a Christian.

The Evangelical Catholic movement is a danger to true Bible Christianity. It promotes ecumenism and stifles evangelisation of Catholics by Protestants. Even genuine evangelicals can be confused in their outreach to Roman Catholics because of the apparent spirituality of some of these people. It is worth bearing in mind that though these people may use Evangelical terminology they will often have a very different understanding of it to you or I. They may speak the language of Zion but they have never so much as had their passport stamped.

Just because someone speaks a particular language it does not make them a citizen of that country. Beware of Evangelical Sounding Catholics! Beware of their 'doctrinal ambiguity'!

CLAIMS OF SPECIAL DISCOVERIES

There have been a multitude of supposed special discoveries belonging to Catholicism documented throughout the centuries. Many are so ridiculous that anyone with an ounce of discernment could see right through the deception, others are shrouded in mystery and myth while others are clearly of human invention, though satanically inspired. These special discoveries range through a variety of artefacts, relics, visions, miraculous statues, wafers, vegetables, and even miraculous buns! *"On October 15, 1996 a customer at the Bongo Java Coffee House in Nashville saw the likeness of Mother Theresa in his breakfast cinnamon bun. Other customers quickly confirmed his discovery!"* One of the comments on the Internet regarding the nun bun was as follows: *"The miracle of the Nun Bun is that it made me smile after a lousy day."* This is about the sum of this so-called miracle, though this is far from being the wackiest!

Some of the better known 'special discoveries' of Rome would include the 'Shroud of Turin', the alleged burial cloth of the Lord Jesus Christ. A clear fraud! Many tests were performed upon the cloth in an attempt to verify its validity; much debate went to and fro on the matter. Why? All that is needed is to view the item in the light of Holy Scripture: the cloth carries an image of a man, including his head, this therefore could not be genuine for the Lord Jesus Christ was buried according to the Jewish rite (see John 19:40) and as such his head was wrapped in a separate cloth from that of his body. (See John 11:44 and 20:7). The Turin shroud is a phoney, a special Catholic discovery.

Others have included enough splinters of the true cross and enough nails from the crucifixion to build Noah's Ark and a series of garden sheds. It is alleged that in AD325 Helena, mother of Constantine, found the seamless coat of Christ. One report read: *"So popular was the relic that hundreds of thousands visited it (during 1891)...many of them were heard to pray as they passed "Holy Coat save me! Holy Coat, pray for me and protect me!" So great was the rush of the faithful that licenses were asked for 1300 new temporary beer saloons and public houses."* Such was the fever of idolatry surrounding this item at that time.

This was but one of twenty-two such coats, all of which were proven to be fraudulent during the 19th century. Many vials of our Lord's blood are claimed to exist, hundreds of bones of this saint and that saint are set in Roman shrines and altars which would include several heads of saint Paul, or was it Peter? Probably both! All of which are of course wonder working! John Calvin, that great Reformer, once wrote 'a Treatise on Relics'.

In it he catalogues a whole array of supposed special discoveries such as these: The brain of St Peter, which proved to be a piece of pumice stone was discovered in Geneva while the head of Mary Magdalene was discovered near Marseilles, later found to be made of 'paper mache'.

Other items mentioned by Calvin include the manger in which Christ was laid and the swaddling clothes in which he was wrapped. The water pots of Cana, and the miraculous wine that our Lord created. In addition there are also numerous special discoveries of Rome and preserved by them for the adoration of the faithful.

The list is almost endless; bread from the Last Supper, the knife used for carving the Paschal Lamb and of course the cup, made of emerald did you know? We must not overlook the towel which the Lord used to wash the disciples feet. Did you know he used three? Each amazingly discovered and preserved in Catholic Mass houses! Speaking of which, did you know that Catholicism discovered a miraculous house! Yes indeed, according to Catholicism, the house in which Mary, Joseph and Jesus lived at Nazareth was flown by angels to Loreto in Italy to prevent it being desecrated by the Turks and because of this 'miracle' Mary was declared the patron saint of aviators!

According to the historian Schaff, the miracles of Catholicism are, *"Unnatural and against reason"*. Calvin would no doubt agree with him. Schaff continues: *"We are told e.g. how St Berinus after being full sail for France, finding that he had forgotten something, walked back dry-shod on the sea; how St Dionysius, after being beheaded took his head in his hand and walked two miles!"*

What absolute nonsense all of this is, but before we move on from this subject we must take a look at Marian apparitions for it is here that Catholicism seems to have a superabundance of 'special discoveries'. We think of places such as Lourdes where a 14 year old child, Bernadette Soubirous, is said to have seen the 'Blessed Virgin Mary' in 1858. Lourdes has since become a popular shrine for Catholic devotion and claims of miracles abound. Another infantile discovery is that of Fatima in Portugal (named after Mohammed's favourite daughter) in 1917 when Mary supposedly appeared to three children aged 10, 9 and 7 years. Again tales of miracles emanating from the site abound.

Strangely though, Pope John Paul II did not see fit to test the healing power of the shrine when he was shot in 1982 but was whisked away to hospital! If there was an ounce of truth in these claims why is it that this Marian Pope, did not seize the opportunity to display her alleged amazing healing powers by entrusting himself to her? What a missed opportunity! Perhaps he too felt that there may be grounds for *"apprehensive concern"* with regard to his impending death.

Of course the greatest special discovery of Catholicism, and its foulest, is the myth of transubstantiation. This dogma of Rome is that which teaches that in the Mass, at the moment the priest pronounces the mystical formula of 'hoc est corpus meum', meaning 'this is my body', the wheaten disc, the Mass wafer, actually becomes the very body, blood, bones and divinity of the Lord Jesus Christ. Not merely a representation of Him, but really Him, called from His throne in Heaven to continue a work which he himself declared was 'finished'!

Dr Elliot relates the following true story of an elderly woman: A Friar one-day came into her cabin, and after the usual salutation he called for a saucepan. Placing the vessel on the fire, with a little water in it, he took out of his pocket a paper containing some flour, which he poured into the pan, making 'stir-about'. When the paste was thickened to the consistency of wax he ordered his host to provide him with two smoothing irons. Having pressed the paste to the thinness of a wafer he then rounded it with scissors and holding it up announced: "When I have consecrated, whoever will not believe it to be the very body blood, soul and divinity of Jesus Christ, will be damned to all eternity".

Such is the christ of Catholicism! Not surprisingly this was the lady's last day as a Catholic for she had seen clear through the nonsense of transubstantiation!

If we consider the weeping, winking, walking, talking, bleeding Madonnas, bleeding hosts, apparitions here there and everywhere, flying houses, wafer gods, tons of miraculous relics, heads, hands, arms, legs etc. We have a lot of, so called, special discoveries all of which demonstrate the cultic nature of Catholicism. None of these Roman 'special discoveries' are anymore valid than Joseph Smith's alleged golden plates upon which Mormonism is built. Both Catholicism and Mormonism are false religions with false foundations and phoney discoveries.

DEFECTIVE CHRISTOLOGY

"In all of the history of the Church, the most grievous heresies have been those which have advocated a view of the person of Christ other than that which is taught in the Word of God" (DB pg. 71).

The christ of Catholicism is not the Christ of the Bible! Rome says: *"Jesus Christ accomplished almost all of the work for our redemption, I would say about 90%"* (Priest Despars). The christ of Catholicism only completed part of the work for salvation, the work that the true Christ himself declared to be finished. Theirs is a finite christ, a cultists christ.

The Christ of the Bible is the perfect Son of God who completed a perfect work upon the cross of Calvary, an infinite work of infinite merit. *"Bearing shame and scoffing rude, in my place condemned He stood, sealed my pardon with His blood. Hallelujah, what a Saviour!"* Only a Christian believer can rejoice in such a way, such words and thoughts of personal assurance are alien to Catholic teaching. It knows nothing of the perfect work of the perfect Saviour. Catholicism further states: *"The guilt of actual sins cannot be transferred from one soul to another. To assert that the guilt of*

81

men's sins was transferred to our Lord dying upon the cross is absurd and blasphemous." (Priest Conway - The Question Box).

The work that the Lord Jesus Christ did for the redemption of His people is deemed by the Roman cult to be *"absurd and blasphemous"*! The Christ of the Bible is the King of Kings, the Lord of Glory, the Mighty God, the Everlasting Father, the Prince of Peace. Omniscient, Omnipotent, Omnipresent, God the creator! The christ of the Roman cult is very different, he is an insipid weakling that must perform the bidding of not only his mother, but that of the priest in the Mass. The priest commands christ to come from the throne of heaven and take upon himself the form of a wafer to be offered as a sacrifice again and again, never able to declare "It is finished"! The christ of Catholicism is defective, as is the finite christ of all the cults, and is a god of their own making.

"Throughout the Latin Church unleavened bread is used at Mass. It is made thin and circular, and bears upon it either the figure of Christ or, the initials I. H. S., and is commonly called 'the wafer'. This is the real christ of the church of Rome, their god and their saviour, and object of worship". (Elliot pg. 175).

What is the Mass? 'Surely it is but an alternative view of the Lord's Supper, or Christian Communion' some

82

will say. There are many both outside the Church of Jesus Christ and within who are under the illusion that the Roman Mass and Christian Communion are the same thing. Are they? Let us examine the matter and discover just who or what the Christ of the Mass is:

On Sunday 7 Dec 97 Mary McAleese, then President of the Irish Republic, partook of the elements in a Church of Ireland communion service. Her actions were seen by many to have been an expression of openness, an ecumenical gesture, a way forward, a bridge building exercise. Others viewed the matter somewhat differently some Protestants and Catholics were outraged, for differing reasons. We saw in the newspapers at the time a great deal of correspondence about the issue, arguing the rights and wrongs of the whole matter. Such was the depth of feeling by some Roman Catholics that Mrs McAleese was branded as a spiritual adulterer, that her actions were akin to one having an extra-marital affair.

It is noticeable that in all of the correspondence that did appear in the papers, there was little of any theological substance, there was very little, from either Protestant or Catholic quarters, which made the point that the Mass and Communion in a Protestant church are two very different things altogether. This is not at all surprising for since the birth of the modern ecumenical movement at the World Missionary Conference at

Edinburgh in 1910 there has been a concerted effort on all fronts to blur all distinctions that exist between Protestantism and Roman Catholicism.

It is perhaps in the doctrine of the Lord's Supper that the greatest differences lie between the two, and so it is here that the most effort has been made by ecumenists to obscure the distinctions. It is interesting to note however that even within Roman Catholicism there are those who have been bold enough to stick to the official line of the Roman Catholic Church and say that *"The blurring of boundaries is no help to the drive for unity"*. Monsignor Denis Faul was quoted in the Irish Times of 9 Dec 97 as saying: *"the whole unity of our church is based around the Eucharist.... while the whole of the Reformation was that their (the Protestant) Eucharist is totally different... Eucharistic intercommunion with Protestant churches was not possible."*

Whilst we may, or may not, agree with Mr Faul, he did toe the official church line. This is also the true Protestant position! What is erroneously referred to as intercommunion is, as the Roman Catholic Archbishop of Dublin stated, *"a sham"*. Such terms as intercommunion, the common usage of the word Eucharist, and some other terminology, all lend weight to the faulty idea that the Roman Catholic Mass and the Lord's Supper are one and the same thing. Nothing could be further from the truth as I hope to be able to demonstrate to you by defining and differentiating between the two. This in turn will clearly demonstrate that the Christ of Catholicism is false.

What then is to be our yardstick in this matter? Evangelical Christians regard the Bible as the sole guide and rule of their faith and that it alone has the final say in all matters of faith and practice. This of course is no more than it claims for itself: *"All scripture is given by inspiration of God, and is profitable for doctrine, for reproof, for correction, for instruction in righteousness".* (1 Tim 3:16). Let us examine what the Roman Catholic church teaches about the Mass and we shall compare that with what the Bible actually teaches concerning the Lord's Supper, or communion. As we continue I believe we shall see that there are great differences between the two. They are different in: Origin, in meaning/symbol, in administration/celebrant, in its recipients and in its effects/benefits.

Let us consider some definitions about the Mass: *"The Sacrifice of the Mass forms a pivot upon which all else turns. If it is what Catholics believe it is, then here is the greatest external manifestation of the love of God for man and the most magnificent testimonial to the validity of Catholicism; but if it be false, it is the worst farce and blasphemy ever perpetrated upon God or man, and the Catholic faith collapses into nothingness."* 'The What and Why of Catholicism', with the imprimatur of the late Cardinal Spellman.

"Let any crumb of the Holy Body which falls to the ground be searched for and if it be found, let the place be scraped should it be of earth and the dust therefrom mixed with water and given to the faithful as a draught of blessing." A Catholic Dictionary of Theology vol 1, pg 9.

"If some people were to ask me, 'where is your God?' I would not have to map out some pilgrimage route to a distant land, but simply point to the Tabernacle." (The box where consecrated wafers are kept). 'Here I Am', Benedictine Convent of Perpetual Adoration.

"During the past few months there have been a number of people leaving the church a few minutes after they have received Holy Communion at 6.15 on First Friday. This is a great dishonour to Our Blessed Lord. The church tells us that Jesus remains in our bodies 15 minutes after we have received communion, that means that our thanksgiving ought to be at least 15 minutes long, and that we should not leave the church until our Lord is no longer with us." 'Church Bulletin', Oakland Calif.

"The sacrifice of the Mass is no mere commemoration of Calvary, but a true and proper act of sacrifice whereby Christ the high priest, by an unbloody immolation offers himself a most acceptable victim to the eternal Father, as he did on the cross." The Catholic Catechism, 1975 John Hardin SJ, pg466.

There we have but a few statements of Catholic belief about the Mass. It is often referred to as Holy Mass, or the Holy Sacrifice of the Mass, and it is at the heart of Roman Catholic theology. Its devotional value for individuals cannot be exaggerated and it is the supreme act of worship upon which, as Cardinal Spellman says, the Roman Catholic church stands or falls! The superstition that surrounds the Mass can be seen in the fact that should a mere crumb of a wafer fall to the ground a search, equal to that of a police manhunt must be made. Catholicism teaches in the Mass that each and every consecrated crumb is in and of itself a whole Christ! If one breaks a wafer into several parts, each part is another christ. If someone should vomit after having received the host, it is to be separated out from the rest and placed in a consecrated place until it is corrupted, because whilst still in the form of a consecrated wafer it is the very body of Christ!

The Roman Catholic Mass is an unbloody renewal, or continuation of the Sacrifice that Christ made upon Calvary and regardless of how different priests might try to vary the way in which they perform the Mass, regardless of what any number of priests might say about the Mass in trying to play down its sacrificial nature, the 'Catechism of Christian Doctrine' as published by the Catholic Truth Society states:

"*Question 274.* Is the Blessed Eucharist a Sacrament only? *The Blessed Sacrament is not a Sacrament only : it is also a sacrifice.*

Question 275. What is a sacrifice? *A sacrifice is the offering of a victim by a priest to God alone, in testimony of his being the sovereign Lord of all things.*

Question 276. What is the sacrifice of the New Law? *The sacrifice of the New Law is the Holy Mass.*

Question 277. What is the Holy Mass? *The Holy Mass is the sacrifice of the Body and the blood of Jesus Christ, really present upon the altar under the appearances of bread and wine, and offered to God for the living and the dead.*

Question 278. Is the Holy Mass one and the same sacrifice with that of the cross? *The Holy Mass is one and the same Sacrifice with that of the cross, inasmuch as Christ, who offered himself, a bleeding victim, on the cross to his heavenly Father, continues to offer himself in an unbloody manner on the altar, through the ministry of his priests.*

There we have it from the horse's mouth the Mass is according to Roman Catholic teaching: An unbloody sacrifice wherein a real victim is offered, that victim is the Lord Jesus Christ who is truly present under the appearance of bread and wine. This sacrifice is a continuation of the work which Christ commenced upon Calvary. It is a continuation of the work of which Jesus Christ himself declared in John 19:30 "It is finished"! It is an *"unbloody"* sacrifice! The scriptures plainly teach: *"without the shedding of blood, there is no remission of sins".*

Heb 10:10ff : *"We are sanctified through the offering of the body of Jesus once.....and every priest standeth daily ministering and offering oftentimes the same sacrifices which can never take away sins: But this man (Jesus) after he had offered one sacrifice for sins forever, sat down on the right hand of God".*

There is some confusion abroad today due to the popularity of what is known as the New Mass that came out of Vatican II. There are those who, mistakenly, think that the Mass has changed in its theology, it has not! It has changed in as much that it is now performed in the language of the country wherein it is being performed, many prayers have been omitted, the priest faces the congregation much more than he previously did, female acolytes are permitted in some churches. Superficial changes have been made but the theology of the Council of Trent, where the Mass was first defined, still stands today having been ratified at all subsequent councils! The latest catechism, published in 1995, merely restates the teaching of Trent also:

"The sacrifice of Christ and the sacrifice of the Eucharist are one single sacrifice: 'The victim is one and the same: the same now offers through the ministry of priests, who then offered himself on the cross; only the manner of offering is different'. 'In this divine sacrifice which is celebrated in the Mass, the same Christ who offered himself once in a bloody manner on the altar of the cross is contained and is offered in an unbloody manner.' Council of Trent (1562): DS 1743; cf Heb 9:14, 27." Catechism of the Catholic Church (1995), pg 307, para 1367.

It is interesting to note here how they refer the reader to Heb 9:14, 27: *"How much more shall the blood of Christ, who through the eternal Spirit offered himself without spot to God, purge your conscience from dead works to serve the living God?...* *"as it is appointed unto men once to die , but after this the judgement:"* How these scriptures are supposed to support the doctrine of the Mass I do not know for they teach of the finished work of Christ. How convenient it is that they fail to direct the reader on to verse 28; *"So Christ was once offered"* or on into Hebrews chapter 10 where we see a clear refutation of the Mass from the scriptures!

Before proceeding to consider the origins of the Roman Mass let us briefly recap: Although the Tridentine Mass has been superseded by the New Mass, that councils teaching on the Mass is still valid. It is essentially:

a) When the words of consecration are pronounced, the elements become the blood, body, bones, soul and divinity of Christ under the appearances of bread and wine. The priest consuming the elements completes the sacrifice.

b) The sacrifice is identical to that of the cross; Christ is both priest and victim in both. The difference is in the manner: bloody upon the cross, unbloody in the Mass.

c) It is a propitiatory sacrifice, atoning for the sins of the living and the dead.

d) Its efficacy is derived from the sacrifice of Calvary, whose superabundant merits it offers to men.

e) The Mass may be celebrated in honour and memory of the saints.

f) Christ instituted the Mass at the Last Supper.

g) The symbols and ceremonies of the Mass were added by the Church, whom God authorised to clothe this ceremony with appropriate decoration.

Anyone who knows anything of Holy Scripture will know that there is not a word in the Bible to support these erroneous claims. Below the reader will discover just where the Mass did originate:

The origins of the Mass: *"In Mithraism a sacred meal of bread and wine was celebrated. Mithraism had a Eucharist, but the idea of a sacred banquet is as old as the human race and existed at all ages and among all peoples."* (The Catholic Encyclopaedia.)

It is within the ancient Babylonian mystery religions that we find the roots of the Roman Catholic Mass. In pagan Rome Cicero spoke of the corn of Ceres and the wine of Bacchus while in ancient Egypt, a cake was consecrated by a priest and was said to become the flesh of Osiris. This cake was then eaten and wine too was consumed as part of the rite. Alexander Hislop, in his book, *'The Two Babylon's*, suggests that the idea of eating a god speaks of how the priests of Ba-al were required to eat human flesh, thus we have 'Cahna-Ba-al', meaning priest of Ba-al, from which we have our word 'cannibal'. It can be seen that the Mass is truly a cannibalistic rite when one considers all that Catholicism teaches concerning it.

The host used in the Roman Mass is deliberately round, it must be a disc, and no other shape will suffice. Why? Because of the origins of the Mass within Mithraism, (Sun worship), which as we have already heard, the Catholic church freely admits to! In the ancient mysteries of Egypt, round cakes were a prominent feature. The higher initiates received a small round cake or wafer of unleavened bread, a representation of the Sun. The ancient Israelites, when they fell into Ba-al worship set up images of the Sun upon their altars, these were the images which the godly young Josiah tore down as we read in 2 Kings chapter 23.

Much of the decor within the Roman Catholic church today is emblazoned with images of the Sun, and all of these speak of its relationship with Mithraism! Even the main altar within St Peter's has these sun images, the host upon the altar is itself a representation of the sun. Consider the shape of a host, the designs upon it of the sun's rays, the IHS which speaks of Isis, Horus, Seb (or Set), the Pagan trinity of the sun god. Consider also the item known as the 'monstrance' wherein the consecrated host is housed for worship, this is itself a representation of the sun!

The Roman Catholic church is a blending together of ancient pagan religion and Christianity, this was brought about by the Emperor Constantine about the year 315 AD. Many pagan practices and beliefs were introduced into the Christian Church, and many Christian practices were paganised! Throughout the early centuries of the, now paganised, Church, there were many varying beliefs concerning the Lord's Supper, and that variety stayed right up until the Council of Trent in the 16th Century.

The first real attempt at formulating a doctrine of 'Transubstantiation' was not until the 9th Century when a monk by the name of Pascasius Radbertus, using the philosophy of Aristotle to support his theories, attempted to explain how something can change in its substance (transubstantiate) without changing in its appearance. Thomas Aquinas later took this matter on board and came up with the expressions of 'substance' and 'accidence' to explain the mystery of transubstantiation.

The Mass defined: It is clearly of pagan origin, and founded upon human tradition and philosophy. It is a cannibalistic rite that has its roots in Mithraism. It is nothing short of witchcraft to suggest that an unregenerate man has the power to command God from his throne in Heaven, turn Him into a wafer and then distribute Him to whomsoever he, the priest, wills. It maligns the fact of the finished work of Jesus Christ upon the cross. Indeed no other proof of the invalidity of the Mass is required than to look at its need to be repeated time and time again. For it is an offering of the same sacrifices which can never take away sins!

The Lord's Supper: It is clear that this whole doctrine of the Roman Mass is very different from that which the Bible teaches regarding the Lord's Supper. How different the spectacle of the Mass is to that of the simplicity of the Christian Communion:

In the Mass the priest performs the following routine, or one very similar: He makes the sign of the cross 16 times, turns towards the congregation 6 times, lifts his eyes to heaven 11 times, kisses the altar 8 times, folds his hands 4 times, strikes his breast 10 times, bows his head 21 times, genuflects 8 times, bows his shoulders 7 times, blesses the altar with the sign of the cross 30 times, lays his hands flat on the altar 29 times, prays secretly 11 times, aloud 13 times; takes the bread and wine and turns it into the body and blood of Christ, covers and uncovers the chalice 10 times, goes to and fro 20 times. Add to all of this the grand vestments, bells, incense and pageantry that go with it and what a striking contrast this all is to the simple memorial meal that Christ instituted as the Lord's Supper! There is no resemblance!

The Lord Jesus Christ commanded that those who love him should take the common elements of bread and wine as aids to remembering His broken body and poured out blood. There was no suggestion that Christians should re-sacrifice him each time they gathered, but rather that they should take the occasion of coming together to ponder upon the completed work of our salvation. Though Protestants vary in the frequency of this memorial, though there are shades of opinion concerning the rightful recipients, and so forth, something that all are agreed upon is that the Lord's table is not a continuation of Calvary, a re-enactment of Calvary nor any such thing, but essentially a simple memorial feast. No matter how grand some Protestants might make the occasion, it remains a memorial meal, and not a sacrifice!

Not only is the Communion *commemorative* of what has been done, it is also *predictive*. In the Communion we not only look back, but forwards to the day when our glorious Lord shall appear to receive us to Himself for all time. *"For as oft as ye eat this bread, and drink this cup, ye proclaim the Lord's death till He come"*. It is furthermore *emblematic*. While it perpetuates the significance of the redemptive work of Christ, the Communion is a teacher of vital Gospel doctrine. It proclaims to the believer the love of Christ, a seal of the Covenant of Grace, and a token of His faithfulness to all those that put their trust in Him. It is not merely a

Communion of the saints, one with the other, but of each person gathered with the one of whom it speaks, the blessed Lord Jesus Christ!

The Communion speaks of the Christian's Spiritual life and nourishment that are derived from Christ, not from the elements, but from Him whom they represent. As natural bread and wine feed the natural body, so Christ 'the Bread of Life' feeds the renewed soul. When Jesus said *"This is my body"* and *"this is my blood"*, he did not mean, nor could have meant, that in a literal sense since both His body and His blood were not in a loaf or a cup but were in His corporeal person. He meant exactly what Protestants have always said he meant, that the elements represented Him. There is therefore *no transubstantiation*, and when received by the communicants, they remain both bread and wine.

There are those in some circles who talk about consecration of bread. Christ blessed God and gave thanks for the bread! The minister's part therefore is but to thank God for the elements, for the glorious realities which they represent, and to ask His blessing upon them as they are applied to a sacred use they do not become holy, they do not take on any mystical or magical qualities. It would be as valid to take any left-over bread and wine and to use them for tomorrow's lunch. They are but common elements emblematical of a spiritual reality.

The greatest contrast between the Lord's Supper and the Mass is that the Mass speaks of a work that is incomplete, something that must be continued. The Communion speaks of the work that has been done, completed, finished, never to be repeated nor continued. Something that has been infinitely done cannot be added to. Such was the work of Christ upon the cross at Calvary. The psalmist, writing prophetically of what Christ would suffer upon the cross, in psalm 22, in the very last clause writes *"He hath done this"*. He wrote of a finished work. Our Lord Jesus, in His agonies upon the cross, declared *"It is finished"* and the writer to the Hebrews writes of a completed work of salvation, and even goes so far as to show how it is that some seek to perpetuate that which has truly been done! (Every priest standeth daily ministering, offering oftentimes the same sacrifices which can never take away sins).

The Scriptures give plain testimony to the fact that the sacrifice of Calvary was a one-time event, never to be repeated, a perfect sacrifice, not to be added to. The Roman Catholic Mass says, no Jesus was wrong, the Scriptures which testify of Him are wrong, come to Mass and continue the sacrifice of Calvary, come along next week and lets do some more!

Who are we to believe? The Word of God, or the words of men? *"To the law and to the testimony, if they speak not according to this Word, there is no light in them."*

Let me remind you of what the late Cardinal Spellman, a man once expected to become Pope said:

"The Sacrifice of the Mass forms a pivot upon which all else turns. If it is what Catholics believe it is, then here is the greatest external manifestation of the love of God for man and the most magnificent testimonial to the validity of Catholicism; but if it be false, it is the worst farce and blasphemy ever perpetrated upon God or man, and the Catholic faith collapses into nothingness."

How right he was! The Mass is the centre of Catholic belief and it is here that the Reformation struck at the heart of the Roman Catholic Church. But she is recovering from that wound, helped along by the ecumenists and liberals. True Christians who will wield once again the Sword of the Spirit, which is the Word of God, must finally put this myth to death! The Mass *is* the worst farce and blasphemy ever perpetrated upon God or man!

Nothing could be clearer, the Roman Catholic Mass and the Christian Communion are indeed, definitely different, the christ of Catholicism is but a finite invention of religious fraudsters while the Christ of the Bible is the Mighty God who did a perfect and mighty work upon the cross of Calvary. A finished, never to be repeated work!

SEGMENTED BIBLICAL ATTENTION

"While we may be fascinated with the words of one of the personalities of Scripture and with the emphasis of a given book of the Bible, we must not fail to pay attention to the message of the entire Word of God" (DB pg. 85).

Some have claimed that the Roman Catholic Church is the mother of the Bible, I heard this claim made during a radio debate in which I was taking part on WMCA New York. Dr Bill Jackson answered this with the statement that: *"if the Catholic church is the mother of the Bible then here is a clear case of child abuse"*.

Here are some examples of that abuse. Below are some excerpts from the Roman Catholic *New Jerome Bible Commentary*. (This has the Imprimatur of Lawrence Cardinal Sheehan. Augustine, Cardinal Bea is the author of the commentary's forward).

1. The Bible contains fiction.
2. Moses did not write the first five books of the Bible. These books came from the J-E-D and P sources centuries after Moses died.
3. The Bible does not predict the coming of the Messiah Jesus Christ.

4. Joshua's account of the destruction of Jericho is fiction.
5. Isaiah did not write Chapters 40-66 of the Book of Isaiah.
6. Isaiah did not predict the coming of Jesus Christ, that he would be born of a virgin, and suffer and die for the sins of all men.
7. The Old Testament does not teach any resurrection from the dead. St. Jerome was wrong when he said Job 19:26 referred to Jesus and the resurrection.
8. The Sixth century B.C. prophet Daniel did not write the Book of Daniel.
9. The Book of Daniel contains errors and fiction.
10. Psalm 16:10 does not refer to the resurrection of Christ.
11. The Books of Ruth, Jonah and Esther are fiction.
12. The Book of Matthew contains fiction.
13. The Ascension of Christ may not be historical.
14. Three thousand were not converted at Pentecost.
15. Paul did not write Colossians, Ephesians, I and II Timothy and Titus.
16. The Bible is not the inspired and inerrant Word of God.
17. Genesis is not historical.
18. Man and the universe gradually evolved from some primary substance.
19. Christian doctrine gradually evolved. The Biblical view of God changed.

20. The Bible contains mythology.
21. The Biblical story of Noah's flood is a myth.
22. Man does not know who the historical Jesus really was.
23. The Gospels are not true history.
24. Jesus was not all knowing.
25. Jesus did not co-exist with the Father from all eternity.
26. Christianity is not the one and only divinely revealed faith.
27. Christ did not die on the cross to appease the wrath of God.

We have seen time and time again Catholicism's awful attitude towards Holy Scripture - it stinks! Not only has she sought to burn and destroy it, to pervert and corrupt its holy pages, to add to it her abominable writings, these entries in the Catholic Encyclopaedia are also very revealing as to how Catholicism views the Bible:

Vol 10, pg.184. *"The Bible as a literary work had traditions that included myth"*.

Vol. 9, pg. 887. *"Some of the miracles recorded in Holy Scripture may be fictional and include imaginative literary creation"*.

Vol. 12, pg. 403. *"The Gospels are not biographies of Jesus and still less scientific history"*.

Such is the Roman cult's view of Holy Writ; therefore, it should come as no great surprise to find that they have a segmented view of the Bible.

Is it not a strange thing for a mother to not know her child? Surely a mother would know every detail and facet of her child, if the child were truly her own! However, Catholicism, professed 'mother of the Bible' has in fact only ever officially defined seven (7) verses of scripture, this is not Protestant propaganda but a statement from an eminent Catholic theologian!

"Many people think that the Church has an official party line on every about every sentence in the Bible. In fact, only seven passages have been definitely interpreted. Even in these few cases, the Church is only defending traditional doctrine and morals. For example Jesus' teaching in John 3:5 that we must be born of water and of the Spirit means that real (natural) water must be used for valid baptism. When Jesus after instituting the Eucharist, commanded his disciples to 'Do this in memory of me', (Luke 22:19; 1 Corinthians 11:24), he meant to confer priestly ordination. Again, the power conferred on the Apostles to bind and loose sins (see John 20:23) authorised them and their successors in the priestly office to forgive sins in God's name. These authoritative interpretations emphasise the biblical origins of sacramental life. The three other defined texts are John 20:22; Romans 5:12 and James

5:14)." (Denver Catholic Register 29/3/98, pg. 10 - Fr FX Cleary SJ).

Notice how the writer merely refers to the final three texts without offering any explanation on such an important matter! He dismisses the fact that Catholicism does not know anything of Scripture, and actually seems to revel in that fact. A cursory look at the above scriptures will show a Catholic segmented view of Scripture, and how they have wrested even these seven from their proper context.

The RC doctrine of the perpetual virginity of Mary is a classic example of Roman Catholic segmented biblical attention. After the fifth century, many excesses of devotion to Mary began to spring up. One was a belief in her perpetual virginity (that Jesus was her only child). One of the reasons for this was to encourage men and women to seek the celibate state as a higher level of spirituality. It came at a time when a decadent society regarded maternity as inferior to virginity. This whole doctrine, of no mean importance, is based upon one solitary verse of scripture.

The scripture used for this is Ezekiel 44:2. *"Then said the Lord unto me; This gate shall be shut, it shall not be opened, and no man shall enter in by it; because the LORD the God of Israel hath entered in by it, therefore it shall be shut."* This is nought but a wicked wresting of the scripture to satisfy their own sordid purposes. If one merely reads the next verse (Ezekiel 44:3) it will be seen that the Catholic application of verse two is a complete nonsense!

Rome's segmented view of holy Scripture is plain for all to see for she picks and chooses those isolated verses which suit her best, often completely out of context, on which to build her erroneous doctrines and dogma. Yet many Roman Catholics insist on trying to perpetuate the myth that Catholicism is a friend of the Bible, and ardent advocate of Bible reading. Nothing is further from the truth. It is upon this issue that Dr Bill Jackson comments in 'the Vatican bank' that "Catholics like to point out that pope Leo XIII granted an indulgence to all of the faithful who would spend 15 minutes reading the Bible with due veneration. This indulgence was for 300 days (Vatican II continued indulgences but removed the time allotment). However, on the flyleaf of the same Bible (New Catholic Edition, Imp. Cardinal Spellman), is a prayer to the Holy Spirit that takes 15 seconds to read. Those who recite (sic) this prayer daily for a month receive a plenary indulgence of five years. Eight minutes of recited prayer = 5 years indulgence; Fifteen minutes of Bible reading = 300 days indulgence."

The Russellites, or Jehovah's Witnesses, so-called, are the experts at this kind of segmented biblical attention.

If you should ever have been so unfortunate as to have these people visit your home you will no doubt have had an encounter something along these lines. They will commence their sales pitch by drawing your attention to just how rotten the world is and lead on to speaking on their interpretation of the future and your part in that. They weave an interesting tapestry before your eyes of what seems to be, to the ignorant, the teaching of the Bible. But it isn't! What they do is just as the Catholics, and other cultists do, they take verses, usually isolated verses, completely out of context and make them a pretext.

The correct way of proceeding to understand what the Bible teaches upon any given subject is to compare verse with verse, allowing the Scripture to be its own interpreter. We must take the teaching of the whole Bible upon an issue and with prayerful consideration, perhaps also looking to great Bible commentators and theologians, come to a sober conclusion concerning the plain teaching of Holy Scripture in its entirety.

ENSLAVING STRUCTURE

"The religious ascendancy of a group of spiritual elitists over the mass of the people is a program and a belief that is hated by God." (DB pg. 93). *"So hast thou also them that hold the doctrine of the Nicolaitans, which thing I hate."* (Rev 2:15).

This text speaks of those that hold sway over a people, having them in subjugation, the practitioners of priestcraft! It speaks of the Roman cult and all those organisations that have a vice like grip upon their followers, owning them mind, body, and soul. A convert to Rome may be required to take an oath such as this: *"I...having before my eyes the Holy Gospels, which I touch with my hand, and knowing that no-one can be saved without that faith which the Holy Catholic Apostolic Roman Church holds, believes and teaches...to which I submit with my whole heart. I believe all the articles that she proposes to my belief, and I reject and condemn all that she rejects and condemns, and I am ready to observe all that she commands me... I believe not only the primacy of honour, but also jurisdiction of the Roman Pontiff."*

He or she further promise to only understand the scriptures as Catholicism dictates and to abide by the dictates of her councils, especially that of the council of Trent!

Catholics must give blind obedience to their cult and its leadership; there can be no room for a free thinker. Free expression, freedom of conscience etc. are alien concepts to Catholicism. It was the practice of papists for many years to insist on pre-nuptial agreements for mixed marriages where the non-Roman Catholic promised to raise his children as Catholics. In every aspect of Catholic life the cult has absolute control, much of which comes through the abuse of the Confessional. It is not only individuals and families that are controlled by this means but whole countries have been subverted through this device.

The questions asked of a young woman in the confessional are too obscene to be written here but the following should give some insight of the enslaving nature of the Confessional: *"I know nothing more corrupting than the law which forces a female to tell her thoughts, desires and most secret feelings and actions to an unmarried priest. The confessional is a school of perdition."* (The Priest the Woman and the Confessional - C Chiniquy).

"If that bond of satanic secrecy which they call the seal, and which is their principle engine for extorting the thoughts of the heart, were to be broken, no female could ever dare to utter to sister, mother, husband, or any human ear, what she has been forced to hear and speak, when stretched on the rack of the Confessional"

Decisions that rightly belong unto a husband and wife would be determined by the Roman cult. For instance, the priest would tell a wife when 'he' thought she had borne enough children. The Catholic priest still holds absolute sway in many Catholic countries today having all the people in subjection and fear through what amounts to spiritual blackmail. This man knows all your darkest secrets because you have told him everything in the confessional, he owns you mind, body, and soul, and the church owns him.

The 'thought police' of this cult are the local priests, though now losing some of their grip in some parts of the world due to various scandals. In Ireland they reigned there with absolute power. Boys playing football would only need to be looked at by a priest to cause them to pick it up and start playing 'Gaelic' instead of the English soccer!

The priest himself is in the grip of Catholicism, they own him completely, and every priest must assent to the syllabus of Pius IX at his ordination. A few extracts will demonstrate further the enslaving organisational structure of the Catholic cult:

"15. No man is free to embrace and profess that religion which he believes to be true, guided by the light of reason! 17. The eternal salvation of any out of the true church of Christ is not even to be hoped for! 24. The church has the power of employing force and of exercising direct and indirect temporal power! 48. Catholics cannot approve of a system of education for youth apart from the Catholic faith, and disjoined from the authority of the church. 53. The civil government may not lend its assistance to any who see to quit the religious life they have undertaken, and to break their vows! 77. The catholic religion shall be held as the only religion of the state, to the exclusion of all other forms of worship."

These few examples clearly demonstrate the enslaving nature of Catholicism, we have not touched upon Nunneries and Monasteries, the six commandments of the church, and the awful fate of those millions who have been put to death for stepping out of line throughout the centuries right up to the present day. But surely extermination of heretics is an ancient relic of Catholicism! Not so, this policy is right up to date - *"The only thing to do with a heretic is to put him to death".* (Fr De Luca SJ - 1901). Don't let anyone fool you into thinking that this kind of Catholic policy is done away with, it's not. The practice of burning Christians may not happen today in 'civilised' countries but it would happen if they could get away with it. Rob Zins has for many years been involved in Roman Catholic evangelism and debating with Catholics. Whilst at one Roman Catholic convention, which Rob was visiting for research purposes, he had opportunity to offer a Catholic priest a copy of his excellent book 'Catholicism'. The response Rob received from the priest was that he could not accept the book, as he would be compelled to burn it! This intrigued Rob, and so, he asked the priest what he would do with him (Rob) if he could, the priests answer was clear as day, *"I would burn you too sir"*.

Rob and many other Bible believing Protestants have no doubt that this priest meant what he said. Catholicism is the most intolerant of all religions and she will ever revert to type when she can get away with it. She will take any steps she can to resist evangelicalism and to hold onto her own adherents, indeed her claim is that once someone is a 'Catholic' they are one forever, regardless of what may be the circumstances. She will not let go of those she has in her clutches and such is her megalomania she will not even reject those whom a dog would be ashamed to acknowledge as its own. Those who have desired to leave for one reason or another have often been the victims of intimidation of this enslaving organisation.

ONE TRUE CHURCH

Rome claims that she is the one true church outside of which there is no salvation however the facts are that this monolithic carbuncle on the backside of humanity is far removed from that which the Lord Jesus Christ intended. Let us examine just how the local church is to be organised with regard to its own internal life and its relationship with other local churches?

"The catholic church is the whole company of those that are elected, redeemed, and in time effectually called from the state of sin and death unto a state of grace, and salvation in Jesus Christ." Cambridge Platform 1648. *"Now ye are the body of Christ, and members in particular."* 1Cor 12:27.

"A church is a congregation of believers in Christ, baptised on a credible profession of faith, and voluntarily associated under special covenant for the maintenance of the worship, the truths, the ordinances, and the discipline of the Gospel." The Church pg 29 H Harvey.

The church is as RB Kuiper states 'The Glorious Body of Christ'. It is glorious in that it is to shine forth as lamp in the darkness of this world. A lamp that does not burn is worthless, and the church is designed to illuminate the hearts and minds of sinners with the Gospel. The church consists of its members, these members are those who have been truly converted unto Christ and have been duly baptised. These members though diverse in the gifts and abilities are one body. One member may be very different to another as the hand is to the eye and yet be firmly united and working for the good of the whole.

This body, the members, should have a say as to who is to be added to their number and who is to be disciplined via the church meeting. The local church is to be a place where the Word of God is faithfully preached, where God is worshipped in spirit and in truth. Where prayer is to be made and where the ordinances are duly observed.

The local church is a part of that 'whole company' consisting of a body of 'called out ones' or 'ecclesia' who covenant together in a visible political union. *"Now therefore ye are no more strangers and foreigners, but fellow citizens with the saints and the household of God; and are built upon the foundation of the apostles and prophets, Jesus Christ Himself being the chief corner stone: In whom all the building fitly framed together groweth unto an holy temple in the Lord: In whom ye are builded together for an habitation of God through the Spirit."* Eph 2:19-22. This union is usually expressed in the 'Church

Covenant' which is an agreement whereby believers consent to give themselves up to the Lord and to the observing of the ordinances of baptism and the Lord's Supper in the same society. *"So we being many, are one body in Christ, and every one members of another."* Rom 12:5.

Kuiper in his book asserts that the church is both a living organism and an organisation (pg 114). A church therefore should be an organised body, living and growing, and this is borne out in scripture: *"Ye also, as lively stones, are built up a spiritual house."* 1Pet 2:5a. Not only does common sense dictate that a house must of necessity be organised else chaos would rule but scripture sets forth that the local church is to be organised. We are exhorted: *"Let all things be done decently and in order."* 1 Cor 14:40. Our God is not a god of confusion and disorder and He has set forth in His Word how the local church is to be organised.

In 1999 the Anglican church adopted a document entitled 'The Gift of Authority'. This document calls upon the adherents of that church to recognise the Bishop of Rome, the Pope, as the head of the Church. This is contrary to Holy Scripture for there is no earthly head of the church of Jesus Christ other than Christ Himself. Christ is the head of the church both visible and invisible, militant and triumphant and it is to Him that each local church is ultimately responsible.

Though Christ is the head of the Church/church He sees fit to rule through the instrumentality of men. Though they represent Him they are always subordinate to Him. As Christ holds the three-fold office of Prophet, Priest and King He has given special offices for the ordering and continued growth of the church in this present world which represent these: The office of Prophet being fulfilled in that of the preacher of His Word, the office of priest being fulfilled in that of the deacon and the office of king in the elders.

The preacher is one who forth-tells the word of God, the deacon's work is one of mercy and compassion whilst the elder is one who rules. These are ministerial offices and *"Officers, instead of making laws for the church, must be content with declaring to it the laws of Christ... Officers of the church may indeed make certain regulations, but such regulations are never comparable to the law of Christ."* Glorious Body of Christ pg 123.

Each believer is, in a sense, an officer in the church and holds the universal office of prophet, priest and king and has a voice in the government of the church. The Heidelberg Catechism sums this up in the question *"Why are you called a Christian?"* and the answer given: *"Because I am a member of Christ by faith, and thus a partaker of His anointing, that I may confess His name, present myself a living sacrifice of thanksgiving to Him, and with a free and good conscience fight against sin and the devil in this life, and hereafter reign with Him eternally over all creatures."* Lord's Day XII, question 32.

This is what is termed 'the universal office'. It belongs to the Christian believer, not the Pope! There are those who hold an extreme view of this universal office, such as some Brethren Assemblies, and they thereby abrogate the special offices of Pastor/Minister, Deacon and Ruling Elder. Special offices are scriptural. Eph 4:11 - 13 speaks of the gift of these to the church and to what end they were given. In Acts 14:23 we read of the ordaining of elders in every church while in Acts 20 the elders of the Ephesian church are called together and charged that they take care of both themselves and the flock! I Tim 5:17 speaks of *"elders that rule well"* and the following verses set forth something of the importance of the preaching office. The members ought to choose their own officers and no-one may impose upon the membership their rule for in a sense it is to be a democracy, though it is in fact a monarchy or Christocracy. The special officers govern with the consent of the membership and they are responsible to Christ as the head of the church. There are those who seem to regard the church meeting as the final authority when it is in fact Christ who is the sovereign head of the church and all things must be in accordance with His Word.

There are four types of church government to be found among the churches these are: Episcopacy, Presbyterianism, Independency and Congregationalism. For many years there has been a clouding of the waters and many churches have a government which is a blending of a number of these. Some confusion has also arisen because there has been a general tendency to equate Independency and Congregationalism as being the same thing which of course they are not. They have similarities but they are quite different.

Episcopalianism is a hierarchical form of church government where a number of bishops lord it over God's heritage without the consultation and consent of the person in the pew taking their authority from a supposed 'apostolic succession'. It is upon this myth that the Papacy is founded and a variety of 'Orthodox' style churches. These would be such as the Eastern, Russian, Greek and Serbian Orthodox churches. These all are of a liturgical form of worship, seemingly more concerned about outward forms than inward grace. More took up with prelacy and pageantry than sinners and Saviour. Such is the nature of Popery and it has no warrant in holy scripture.

Presbyterianism also adds to the Word of God going beyond the regulative principle in matters of church government. Again there is neither consultation with, nor consent of the people in the pew and all decisions are taken via a number of committees that are made up of elders and ministers. Presbyterianism, like Episcopalianism, creates an 'us and them' situation, of clergy and laity, an unscriptural position.

The Congregational order is that which is usually found among the various free churches and it is that form of church government where the seat of power resides with the people in the church meeting, a form of democracy. Extreme forms of Congregationalism lead to anarchy, factionalism, cliques and divisiveness. Brethrenism is a form of Congregationalism and is often quite anarchic in its outworking. Of the three forms of church government mentioned so far, Congregationalism is the nearest to the biblical pattern, however, as stated, it does have its faults and the reason for this is that it too falls short of the biblical pattern.

The form of church government set forth in Scripture is that of true Independency where the elders rule by consent of the people. This is the historical position of the Particular Baptists, generally referred to today as Reformed Baptists.

Scripture teaches autonomy of the local church as held to by Independency, this can be seen in a number of ways:

"(i) The pattern of rule established by God for His people in biblical times. God's people have always been governed as visible entities, or congregations.

(ii) The direct teaching of our Lord on church government. Matthew18:15-20 shows that the church is the final court of appeal in disciplinary matters. There is no authority or power upon earth that is higher than that given by Christ to His church.

(iii) The final teaching of the book of Revelation. The vision of the lampstands in Chapters 1 to 3 show that congregations should be independent and autonomous." (Keys of the Kingdom pg 62 Poh Boon Sing.)

Not only is the church to have autonomy from other churches but, recognising that Christ is the head of the Church the biblical position with regard to the relationship of Church and State is to be that of Voluntarism. i.e.: The belief that both church and state are equal and independent, each with its own God given sphere of jurisdiction. Some Presbyterians and Reformed Baptists tend to hold to this position whilst others hold to extremes either side of this position.

The biblical position of Elders ruling by consent of the congregation is plainly taught in Scripture. Elders, as representatives of Christ, are overseers of the church

(Acts 20:17,28. 1 Tim 3:1-7, Titus 1:5-9.). The work of ruling/governing the church is specifically theirs and the members are expected to submit to the elders through obedience and respect. (Hebrews 13:7, 17. 1 Thess 5:12.).

John Owen said: *"The rule and government of the church, or the execution of the authority of Christ therein, is in the hand of the elders. All elders in office rule, and none have rule in the church but elders."* Vol 16 pg 106.

The relationship between Elders and Deacons is dealt with by another statement by John Owen: *"The care of the whole church, in all its concernments, is principally committed unto the pastors, teachers, and ruling elders, it is the duty of the deacons, in the discharge of their office, - (i) To acquaint them from time to time with the state of the church, and especially of the poor, so far as it falls under their inspection; (ii) To seek and take their advice in matters of greater importance relating to their office; (iii) To be assisting unto them in all the outward concerns of the church."* Vol 16 pg 151.

The authority to govern the church belongs to the elders, not the deacons. The office of deacon is subordinate to that of elder. The rule of elders is denied by both Congregationalism and Episcopacy whilst both Independency and Presbyterianism recognise its validity. Priests do not come into the reckoning at all being but another papist invention designed for the subjugation of the people in the pew.

There are those who advocate a parity or equality between the elders of a church, they are in error for whilst it is true that all elders must be able to teach not all elders are pastors. The office of pastor is to have the primacy in the church, teaching elders have priority over the ruling elders. All pastors are elders, but all elders are not pastors. The elders are to be appointed via 'popular election', It is popular because the people, the church members make their choice, and it is election because they choose of suitably qualified men under the guidance of the existing elders. Deacons are similarly elected and the qualifications are similar too, though they are not required to be able to teach. The day to day business of the church is left in the hands of the elders and deacons to conduct as per their mandate given them via the church meeting. It is in the church meeting that the weightier matters are considered, the advice of the elders sought and the consent of the members given, or not as the case might be.

I have by no means exhausted this subject, though I have perhaps exhausted the reader on this point and it shall therefore suffice me to say that it is as clear as day that the organisation that is known as the Roman Catholic Church is no church at all, except that of

Satan. It in no way resembles a Christian church as taught by the Bible but is an enslaving organisation which is concerned about the control of people and their wealth rather than the Gospel of Jesus Christ.

Let us conclude this matter with a brief look at the relationship between the local church and other churches and perhaps hold in mind Rome's attitude to these things:

The visible church is an autonomous collective, each church having the right to govern its own affairs without interference from any outside agencies. There are however strong ties between all that are truly the saints of God and we should seek to encourage fellowship between them, yet exercising great care in regard to those who tolerate error. There should be clear biblical separation from those who are apostates, unbiblical or compromised. (2 Corinthians 6:14ff).

Likeminded churches should seek to support one another in both spiritual and practical matters, e.g. prayer and finances, evangelism etc. Thereby demonstrating our love and affinity. There should be communication concerning important matters, I include here the recognition of another church's discipline of its members. We should seek to uphold their censure, except in a case where, consultation having been made, it is found to be contrary to Scripture.

There are those who advocate assemblies of messengers and other associations of churches in an effort to assist one another in various matters whilst seeking to maintain autonomy. This would perhaps be a profitable thing but would only work among churches of a like mind for how can two walk together except they be agreed? Loose associations such as those where only a basic statement of faith is to be agreed upon for membership is a recipe for disaster in these ecumenical days when there are Evangelical sounding Catholics and other cultists seeking to infiltrate the Church.

The sole guide and rule of our faith is to be the Holy Scriptures, the yardstick by which we must measure is the Bible and those whom we might seek to fellowship with must likewise have the same standard for: *"If they speak not according to this word (the Word of God) it is because there is no light in them."* Isaiah 8:20. There is no light in Catholicism, it is a wicked despotic system of demonic design.

124

FINANCIAL EXPLOITATION

"An almost universal characteristic of the cults is an insatiable financial appetite in the leadership." (DB pg. 101).

No surprises here, Catholicism is in the frame again! In the Irish Republic the saying is: High money - High Mass, low money - low mass, no money - no mass. This unholy Roman cult doesn't give anything away free of charge, no small wonder that it has all the riches that it does have. Papa is well looked after, flash cars, sumptuous palaces etc. Well, what else for 'God on earth'?

Catholicism is filthy rich and ever desiring more, but where does she get it all from? Primarily the purse and pocket of the gullible and religiously bewildered who have swallowed the mummery and tripe of the priest and have given their money, perhaps their last penny, for masses to be said on behalf of deceased loved ones. Others have paid out for their very own saint to place on the mantle at home, while others have given money for a candle to be lit, which, it has been known for the priest to extinguish as soon as the purchaser is out of sight!

Rome has a thousand and one money making rackets designed to exploit her followers; indeed the Vatican itself was built via the sale of indulgences during the 16th century. It was this money making racket that Martin Luther exposed with his ninety-five theses, the scam was revealed for what it was and a great reformation ensued. Rome is the great queen of money making scams from shrines to lottery tickets she exploits her followers financially. Whilst on a visit to the USA I visited the shrine of 'Our Lady of La Salette", and though it was winter, and not many 'pilgrims' were about, one could see the various rackets in full swing: Light a candle for X amount, buy a Mass for X amount, buy any one of a whole array of idols, pictures, scapulas and such in the souvenir shop for X amount, visit the Stations of the Cross, not forgetting to place your offering in the box at the end. Climb up the replica 'Scala Santa', the holy stairs (a supposed replica of the staircase which Christ ascended to Pilate), how interesting, another collection box! At the time I visited they were even holding a lottery for a car! (No, I didn't buy a ticket).

How sad all of this is, those giving to Catholic schemes just do not realise that they are being fleeced, they actually think they are helping their salvation by purchasing these sacraments and sacramentals. Those in poorer countries don't get off any lighter, for Catholicism will extract the last penny from the widow's purse if she can. Many think that the Maxwell pension fraud of the 1990s was terrible, and so it was, but Catholicism's fraudulent dealings are carried out every day upon poor unsuspecting and deluded people, and they continue to get away with it scot-free! It is Catholicism's financial exploitation of people that lies behind the oft quoted retort of the sceptic 'religion! - it's just a money making racket!' How very true this is of the Catholic cult. Within this cult there are several other cults such as the cult of Mary and that of Padre Pio. Both of these are money-making rackets and have their own memorabilia shops and outlets much like the bigger football clubs such as Manchester United.

Merchandising is their main business, they want to sell hope to their victims via the sale of masses, statues, medals, indulgences, videos, relics, rosaries, scapulars, posters, and candles. Magazine subscriptions, cult subscriptions, pilgrimages etc. The Bible tells us that *"there is a way which seemeth right unto a man, but the end thereof are the ways of death"*. None of these things can bring salvation to lost souls.

As sordid as it is for the big football clubs to charge their supporters extortionate amounts of money for the latest team shirt or kit they are not as bad as the Roman cult. To my knowledge Man Utd or Liverpool FC do not make any miraculous claims for the wearing of their shirts, they do not give any false hope concerning the future life. They simply say here is yet another very expensive new football kit, buy it if you are stupid enough. Catholicism on the other hand does, as we have seen, make all kinds of claims in an effort to con the gullible into purchasing over-priced garbage.

I recall an RC newspaper advertising the sale of kits to help someone sell their house. Out of curiosity I bought one. In the box I received a small statue of St Joseph and instructions on how to sell my home through this statue. Basically the idea was that you dug a hole near the base of the 'For Sale' sign and then buried the statue head down in the hole with words to the effect of ' dear St Joseph please sell our house as we will not dig you up until you do so. The claim was made that this would sell your house in a very short period of time, as St Joseph doesn't like being buried upside down! How's that for extortion? How's that for financial exploitation?

Then of course there is the blatant robbery and defrauding of those unfortunate enough to have been placed under the care of one of Rome's children's homes or hostels. There is the defrauding of those who have entered in upon holy orders into nunneries and monasteries by having them sign blank deeds of covenant and extracting promises that all worldly good will be handed over to the church. Though one might possess a reasonable amount in the bank on entering a Catholic institution or order you can be sure that there won't be a penny there when, or if, that person should ever decide to leave. This stripping newcomers of all that they possess is common among the more fanatical cults but the world seems to think such practices are acceptable when it is Catholicism that is doing the fleecing. For evidence of these wicked practices see such publications as 'The Awful Disclosures of Maria Monk' or 'Paganry, Popery and Pillage'. The wholesale robbery of those entrusted to the care of the Roman system is clearly documented and is beyond refutation.

DENUNCIATION OF OTHERS

"When one announces himself as the true messiah, all others of course are false and must be put down." (DB pg. 103).

If Rome is the one true church outside of which there is no salvation, as they claim, then of course all others are heretical. We already know what Rome does to heretics, or would like to do! Her wicked deeds against those who have dared to differ with her are well documented in the annals of history. We think of the Albigenses, Paulicians, Waldenses, the Lollards of England, etc., etc. *"A Noble Army of Heretics"* as one rightly put it.

Even today in countries where Catholicism has control those who oppose her are shot, burned out in the night, terrorised by the mother of cults. Look at the past fifty years in Ulster. Those evil deeds of the IRA and other nationalist terror groups were carried out with the full blessing of 'Holy Mother Church'. IRA prisoners, enemies of the state, murderous criminals were rewarded for their evil deeds with gold crucifixes from the pope! Never were the acts of the IRA officially condemned during the campaign of violence and it is quite remarkable that the voice of Catholicism in objection to violence has only ever been heard when Catholics have been the victims. I suspect that had the awful atrocity of the Omagh bomb only killed Protestants, then there would not have been much reaction of horror, regret or condemnation from official Catholic sources. As it was, many of the poor victims of that evil deed were Catholics, and Catholic children at that, hence the outrage, and quite rightly too!

What of those slaughtered by the inquisition, or the St Bartholomew's Day massacre in France when 70,000 Protestant men, women, and children were slaughtered. Dare we forget the 'Convert or Die' policy in Yugoslavia during World War II where thousands were put to death at the hands of Roman Catholic militia. What of the Anabaptists of Europe at the Reformation? Let us not forget those who are suffering under her tyranny in parts of the world today in all continents. Spare a thought for the thousands murdered and maimed by the Roman Catholic IRA in Northern Ireland, Britain and Europe. Gerry Adams, a member of the IRA Army Council, was once asked "How far are you prepared to go Gerry?" His reply was "I am prepared to wade up to my knees in Protestant blood for a united Ireland!" Such attitudes are not merely the satanic tendencies of some individuals who happen to be Roman Catholics; statements such as this by the psychopathic Adams are the official line of the Vatican.

Some have estimated that the total number of deaths so far through the ages due to Catholic persecutions is in the region of fifty million so wading up to the knees in Protestant blood will be to them but a drop in the ocean! After all, heretics are expendable!

The title of this chapter might be better entitled 'Murderous Tendencies'! One only need consider such a book such as *"The Teaching of the Catholic Church"* by Karl Rahner, an eminent Roman Catholic theologian, to discover this to be true, for therein you would find a whole array of curses pronounced upon those who differ in any point of doctrine with her. Great men such as Luther, Calvin, Zwingli, and Huss are condemned and cursed by Rome. Such curses are official pronouncements of Catholicism known as 'anathema' and these are spewed out time and again against those who take the side of Holy Scripture. Indeed, Vatican II describes those who love the Word of God as *"almost a cult"!* (Decree on Ecumenism). Rome today sometimes refers to those who differ with her as being 'separated brethren' rather than 'heretics'. Perhaps the entry in a Catholic dictionary might more correctly read 'For separated brethren see target'! For this is certainly still her true attitude and position with regard to her opponents.

At a debate which was taking place in Oxford University in November 1967 between Ian Paisley and the Roman Catholic Member of Parliament Norman St John-Stevas Mr Stevas announced to the world regarding Mr Paisley *"I don't say shoot him. I don't say not to shoot him - But if you are going to shoot him - shoot straight."* This was a blatant attempt to incite Roman Catholics to murder and a classic case of Rome's denunciation of others.

If Rome's denunciation was merely verbal rhetoric it would not be worth taking too much notice. Unfortunately, for the millions of her victims, Catholic denunciation meant a death sentence. This is documented in such publications as Monica Farrell's 'Ravening Wolves' where we find records such as this taken from a chapter of 'Freedom's Foe' by Pigott entitled "The Cruelty of the Roman catholic Church". These excerpts are included in particular due to the current conflict in the Balkans but many other atrocities are documented in Pigott's book:

"In early 1941 Yugoslavia (then neutral) contained a medley of religions (such as Orthodox Church, Roman Catholic, Moslem and Jewish-and there were a number of gypsies). In one of the northern provinces, Croatia, there happened to be a preponderance of Catholics over the assorted "heretics." And there was, of course, the usual Catholic Action organisation, a well-drilled fifth column, ready and willing to obey any papal commands.

In early 1941, to the lantern-jawed Italian schemers inside the Vatican, Yugoslavia appeared to be a weak country; and a thousand miles away from her only possible ally, Great Britain. And, inside Yugoslavia there was the key province of Croatia where there was a number of Catholic Action quisling fanatics: (there was also a minority of apparently defenceless heretics ripe for extermination or forcible conversion to the "One True Church "). For the Back Room Boys of the heresy-hunting department, it was indeed a tempting situation, full of very wonderful possibilities.

When Hitler invaded Yugoslavia all patriots were called upon to defend their homeland. The Roman Catholic Croats promptly declined to do so; in fact they proclaimed an independent Government and, encouraged by the Vatican and Catholic Action, they turned out in force to welcome the German invaders and did everything possible to hinder and embarrass the loyalists: much the same sort of thing had happened previously in 1940 when the Catholic Rexists helped the Nazis into Belgium and the Catholic Vichyists facilitated their operations in France. As soon as the Germans and Italians reached Croatia, a " Holy War " was started against heretics.

Archbishop Stepinac was Vicar General of the traitor army. Led by fanatical monks and friars (carrying knives as well as crucifixes), the members of the

Catholic Action embarked on an orgy of horror and bloodletting which had not been seen in Europe for 1,500 years. The dagger bearing clerics promised Absolution for any atrocities committed against the heretics, and the holy men personally participated in the atrocities and wielded their weapons as actively as the civilian murderers. One Franciscan monk named Filipovic admitted that, after killing his first victim (who was a child), he had told his fellow Quislings, "I re-christen this degenerate in the name of God. You follow my example and kill." 1,500 Serbs were killed that day in the town alone. Later, this villain was made a Camp Commandant, and admitted that he had ordered the murder of thousands of men, women and children.

A favourite method was to drive the Serbs inside an Orthodox Church, bolt the doors and then set the building on fire. ("Eastern Approaches" by F. MacLean). *Hundreds of thousands of Croatia's Serbs Moslems, Jews and bewildered gypsies were rounded up and condemned to death, torture or mutilation. Orthodox Churches were burnt down; in some cases sons were compelled to assault their own mothers before the altars. In winter, victims were driven on to the frozen rivers and were plunged to death through holes made in the ice. Expectant mothers had their bodies ripped open by Catholic daggers. At a place called Nevesinje, a Serb family of father, mother and four, children were captured by Catholic brutes. The mother and the children were kept together and starved for a week, and then a savoury dish of roast meat was brought in to them; naturally they ate ravenously enough and then they were callously informed that they had just eaten some of their husband and father.*

Peter Brzica, a law student, who had attended a Franciscan college, was a member of the Catholic Order of Crusaders. He was one of the Quislings in control of the concentration camp at Jasenovac in August, 1942, when orders were issued to liquidate many victims. Bets were made as to who could kill the largest number of inmates; and, with a specially sharp butcher's knife, Brzica cut the throats of no fewer than 1,360 Yugo-Slav prisoners, his own countrymen. Having been proclaimed the prize-winner of the competition, he was elected to be "The king of the Cut-throats," and his other rewards included a gold watch, some wine and a roasted sucking-pig. This awful episode has been duly authenticated and is included in a book which was written about the concentration camp at Jasenovac. ("Terror over Yugoslavia " by Avro Manhattan).

These are some of the actions which the agents of "The Holy Catholic Church" use in their 20th century efforts to stamp out its rivals. These horrors were deliberately committed in the name of Christianity by the agents of the Vatican which, in 1956, (and now in 1999), howls so vociferously regarding the alleged intolerance of others. Even the Germans and Italians were often nauseated by what the Croats did: (they are an unusually cruel race with a reputation dating back to the Thirty Years War-1618-1648-when the Pope summoned them up to fight against the German Protestants. "From cholera, hunger and the Croats, may the good Lord deliver us," was a German Protestant prayer)."

If any should require further evidence of the persecuting nature of Catholicism a perusal of an excellent book by J McDonald entitled "Catholicism Analysed" has a chapter on "The Church of Rome and Persecution", some extracts of which appear below.

"Q. 1. Has the Church of Rome ever resorted to persecution?
A. She has done so in every Country and in every age in which she has had the power.

Q. 2. Has not persecution been merely an incidental fact in her history, chargeable against individual members only, but for which she herself cannot be held accountable?
A. No. Persecution has been, and still is, the authorised creed of the Church of Rome, expressly laid down by the infallible decrees of Popes and Councils,

avowedly taught by her doctors and professors, and persistently enforced whenever and wherever she has had the power.

Q. 3. What fact seals Rome's responsibility for the persecutions of the past *?*

A. The fact that she has never expressed regret for, or repudiated, those persecutions, and that she still carries out the same creed, as far as she can and dare.

Q4. Have any Popes ever published bills, expressly enjoining the extermination of heretics?

A. Yes. Pope Urban II, so early as 1088, decreed that "Those are not to be accounted murderers or homicides, who, when burning with love or zeal for their Catholic Mother against excommunicated persons, shall happen to kill a few of them "; this was embodied in the Canon Law of Rome as Cause xxii., quest. v., chap. 47, Excommunicamus, and made an article of faith. Urban was followed by Honorius II., Alexander IV., Urban IV., Clement IV., Nicholas III., and many others, all of whom, in turn published bulls for the suppression and extermination of heretics.

Q. 5. Did Pius IX. endorse this persecuting creed?

A. In his Allocution of September 1851 he declared that every other worship than the Roman Catholic worship must be banished and interdicted. In his Encyclical and Syllabus of 1864 he denounced liberty

138

of conscience as insanity, and freedom of speech as the liberty of perdition; and he anathematised those who denied 11 that the Church had a right to employ force. "

Q6. Is Leo XIII. of the same spirit?

*A. Yes. He granted to the Cardinal Archbishop of Toledo, in Spain, a brief, forbidding any Spaniard, under pain of excommunication, to give either food or shelter to any Protestant missionary; and lie addressed an autograph letter to King Alphonso, begging him to use every effort of the civil power to banish 1'rotestaiit missionaries, and to confiscate their churches, schools, etc., even in violation of the Spanish Constitution. In the same spirit he excommunicated all who had anything to do, directly or indirectly, with the building of Protestant places of worship in Rome, or who, out of curiosity, went to a Protestant service; and he expressed his regret that he had not the power to suppress Protestant churches and schools altogether.'
In his Encyclical, "Immortalae Dei" he looks back to the ages of persecution with regret as unhappily past, and would fain see them return again.*

Q, 7. Have any Councils of the Church promulgated the same creed?

A. Yes. The fourth Council of Lateran (in a decree, repudiated by Keenan, but acknowledged in the Maynooth College Text Books), under the presidency of Pope Innocent III, anathematised all heretics, and enjoined that after condemnation they should be delivered over to the secular arm; it decreed also that the secular powers of all ranks and degrees should exert themselves to extirpate all heretics found in their territories. It was in pursuance of this decree that the Emperor Frederick II published his Edict in regard to the heretics in his dominions, in which he says, "We shall not suffer these wretches to live who infect the world by their seducing doctrines, and who, being themselves corrupted, more grievously taint the flock of the faithful."

Q. 8. What utterance did the Council of Trent give on the subject?

A. After declaring that all baptised persons are bound to observe the precepts of the Church, it added, that " If anyone should say that such as are unwilling to do so are to be left to their own choice, and not to be compelled to lead a Christian life (that is, conform in all things to Rome) by any other punishment than exclusion from the Eucharist and other sacraments until they repent, let him be anathema.' It also called on secular princes to enforce this decree."

These are but a few of the many discussions upon this question in McDonald's book. It may be of interest to the reader to learn that the pronouncements of the Council of Trent are still valid today having been ratified as recently as Vatican II, they are not, as some would have the public believe, ancient history.

SYNCRETISM

Syncretism is a blending together of various religions, a kind of theological soup. Cults like to shop around and take this bit from here and that bit from there and then tie it all together with some human reasoning. Catholicism is no different! When one considers the very origins of Catholicism, how it was formed out of a blending together during the fourth century of a paganised Christianity and a supposedly Christianised paganism. Constantine never was a Christian, but he was very much the means of bringing into being the Roman cult, his state religion.

Rome's attitude has often been that of, if you can't beat them, assimilate them, absorb them. This is their secondary tactic for heretics, if there are too many to burn or bomb, take them by stealth. On a trip to Peru in 2008 I saw first-hand evidence of the blending together of Catholicism with the indigenous beliefs. In fact the tour guide made a point of it and referred to the fact quite openly when we paused to view an ancient RC church in the region of Arequipa. Common ground is being sought today by Rome among all those whom she has previously sought to wipe off the face of the earth. She is working towards relationships with Judaism,

Islam, and Protestant churches, she is also making motions towards all the major cults, seeking dialogue. No doubt she will find much in common with the Mormons, Jehovah's Witnesses etc., they being cults also! Hindus, Sikhs, Animists, Mithraists etc. are all on her menu, all are being wooed into her clutches.

We are told today that we should forget that which divides us and concentrate on those things that unite us. That should be real easy for Bible Protestants because we have absolutely nothing in common with Catholicism! She is the spawn of Satan and we will have no part in her, and she has no part in us.

"Pope John Paul II said that the Roman Catholic Church accepted the truth and goodness found in Islam, Hinduism and Buddhism. He invited their adherents to common prayer that mutual understanding may grow and moral values be strengthened. ...The Vatican Council made it clear that other Christians, Jews non-Christians and atheists can be saved and are united to the church as the people of God in varying degrees." (Christians Guide to Roman Catholicism pg. 48). Catholicism is ever seeking to build a new tower of Babel, it very own tower of power, and syncretism is but another tool that she is using to build her ecumenical super-church.

Chester Todd wrote in his book "*The Case Against Modernism*": *A world religion is on the way which will be more religious than Christian. It will be human rather than divine, it will be natural rather than supernatural. Its god will be its servant, not its sovereign, its Christ will be its leader not its king. Its political economy will be a democracy not a theocracy, its saints will be its socialists not its seers. Its goal will be a human utopia not the kingdom of the coming king. This coming world religion is envisioned by liberals as the harbinger of the kingdom but by biblical writers as the forerunner of Antichrist.*"

"*That world religion is the final flock of Satan's religious activity*" says Dr Bill Jackson of Christians Evangelising Catholics. This world religion is that which the 'Ecumenical Movement' is being steered towards with Satan at the helm. The Greek word from which we have the English word 'ecumenical' is 'oikumene', meaning 'world' and the 'Ecumenical Movement' is a movement towards a world religion.

In II Thessalonians 2:7 we read that "*The mystery of iniquity doth already work.*" The Ecumenical Movement is a major player in this mystery of iniquity which is the direct opposite of the "*Mystery of godliness*" of which we also read in scripture.(I Tim 3:16). Throughout the ages these two great mysteries have militated one against the other since eternity past and shall continue to do so until the last day when Satan shall finally be cast down. (Rev 20:10).

Satan has ever desired to dethrone God and enthrone himself, it is his boast that he shall be like the Most High (Isaiah 14:12-14). By becoming like God he would effectively dethrone Him for there cannot be two supreme beings. In Isaiah 14:14 he declares war upon God but even Satan knew that he couldn't attack God head on so he set forth to do what he considered the next best thing, attack God's creation, and especially the pinnacle of it, man. His first attack came in the garden of Eden when he caused Adam and Eve to sin. He had told them "*Ye shall be as gods*", "*You will be like God*" (Gen 3:5).

To elevate man and thereby degrade God has ever been Satan's ploy that he might at least seem to be on an equal footing with God. We are in a battle and though it would seem that in Eden Satan won round one we know from scripture that God will defeat Satan, indeed He already has done so when Christ died and rose again but Satan being the proud boaster that he is he doesn't seem to know it yet. (Ezek 28:2-19). Satan knows that man is a religious being and has a desire to worship, he could discern this merely from watching Cain for even he brought an offering, albeit an unacceptable one. Satan knows that man will either worship the God that created him or a god he has created. Therefore Satan devised an alternative god for man to worship, he has developed a means of leading men wholesale away from God whilst giving them the impression that they were following Him. He does this by means of counterfeit religion.

Ecumenism is a vehicle for the furtherance of false religions such as the various eastern philosophies, cults, humanism, Catholicism and Liberation Theologies. Babel was Satan's first ecumenical enterprise. Babel was a religious society that sought to ascend into the Heavens by their way. They had their own god, and their own saviour, and they had an outward unity such as the present day ecumaniacs are seeking, but it was counterfeit and God destroyed it all. Today's ecumenism is seeking to build another Babel and their god is a conglomeration of many gods, a syncretistic mash of human religion. God will deal with this second Babel as He did with the first.

During the 20th century the ecumenical machinations of Satan have been seen in such things as 'The World Missionary Conference' of Edinburgh in 1910, 'The Life and Work Conference' of Stockholm 1925 and Oxford 1937. The slogan of the latter was "*Doctrine divides, service unites*". This translated means something like it doesn't matter what you believe so long as we can do things together. This is precisely the attitude of the ecumenical gatherings of the present day, unity at any price, even at the expense of the one true and glorious Gospel of our God. As ecumenism waxes stronger and stronger, evangelism of Catholics and other 'Religious but Lost' people wanes and it would appear to evangelical Christians that Satan will win the battle. As this ecumenical movement develops into the Satanic super church there are more and more seen to fall away from Bible Christianity and it is a sure indication that we are indeed in the period which the Bible describes as the last days.

This ecumenical soup of religions is working itself out in three ways: Philosophically, structurally and practically.

Philosophically via the teachings of eastern religions and what is termed 'New Age' teachings. Since the 1960s these have been increasing in popularity among the churched and unchurched in both Europe and the Americas. All denominations have been infiltrated and influenced by these Satanic teachings. Transcendental Meditation, Silver Mind Control techniques and Yoga are common practices among many who claim to be Christian. There are many who have led many people astray into occult practices wrapped in the guise of Christian spirituality. The underlying theme of the New Age is that of "*Ye shall be as gods*". New Age practices and philosophies point to self-fulfilment, self-esteem and being the master of one's own destiny. Once this is attained God is dethroned and man enthroned.

Structurally the Roman Catholic church has the organisation to bring about Satan's designs for a one world super church. Since Vatican II, convened in1962 under Pope John XXIII and closed in 1965 under Paul VI, the Roman Catholic church has been making ecumenical movements towards the Greek Orthodox, Anglicans, Jews, Communists, Islam, Hinduism, and even Mormons. Rome has worked very hard over the past 30 years or so to convince protestants, those who stand for biblical truth, that she has changed and such has been her success that a leading Pentecostal figure, David du Plessis, at the Jesus 1979 rally in San Francisco stated:

"We used to be called heretics but now we are called separated brethren. That was a wonderful act of forgiveness by the Holy Father". Protestants, real and supposed, are being sucked in to the ecumenical movement as are many false religions.

Rome today has had spiritual associations with most of the world's religions and accepts, at least outwardly, that they are valid ways to God. All of these were invited to pray with John Paul II at a gathering in Assisi in recent years: Christians, Moslems, Buddhists, Hindus, Jews, African Animists, Sikhs, Ba Hai,

Zoroastrians, Shinto, Janes, and Mithraists. The ploy to bring them together was peace. Ecumenism's cry of a false peace has often been heard: "*Peace, peace, when there is no peace*". Jesus came not to bring an earthly peace but a sword! A sword of truth, a sword which to one is a savour unto life and to another a savour unto death. He came to divide the nations, to separate out His people from the world by the Sword of the Spirit, which is the Word of God.

Practically, i.e. the means or vehicle for this ecumenical movement is primarily, I am sorry to have to say, the Charismatic movement, and more recently the 'Evangelicals and Catholics Together' movement. The Charismatic Movement suits Satan's needs very well as a means of carrying forth his plans and it fits in well with both the philosophical and structural aspects. Charismatic teaching became resurgent during the 1950s and its great appeal is that it matters little to some less discerning Christians what one believes doctrinally, the important thing is 'experience'. Even charismatic Christians need to know what they believe and why they believe it. It was Cardinal Augustin Bea, Jesuit Confessor to Pius XII and a key figure behind John XXIII who paved the way for Roman Catholic charismatic renewal by inviting David du Plessis to the final session of Vatican II and shortly afterwards Roman Catholic Charismatic Renewal was born in 1967 at Duquesne University, Pittsburgh, USA.

In 1981 Fr Tom Forrest was appointed Director of the 'International Charismatic Catholic Renewal Office', he was also appointed as director of the next Roman 'wooden horse', the so-called 'Decade of Evangelism'. Gullible protestants got the idea into their heads that if Rome was evangelising then we didn't need to evangelise them. But what sort of evangelism was Rome about, and is she about? Tom Forrest leaves us in no doubt for at a training session for Roman Catholics at Indianapolis 90 he stated: "*My job, my role, our role in evangelisation is not just to make Christians. Our job is to make people as richly and fully Christian as we can make them by bringing them into the Catholic Church....No you don't just invite someone to be a Christian. You invite them to become Catholics.....We're ten years short of 2000 years, and our job is to use this remaining decade evangelising everyone we can into the Catholic Church, into the body of Christ, and into the third millennium of Catholic history.*"

Just three years earlier in New Orleans a wide spectrum of Neo-Pentecostal groups, Youth With A Mission, Baptists, Mennonites, Lutherans and others joined together with Roman Catholics, the underlying factor for this unity was one of charismatic experience.

The 'Blessed Virgin Mary' features very much in the ecumenical process and is a common link with many other false religions, especially those that have their own female deities. She is considered by many to be the gate to charismatic gifts and is a symbol of ecumenism, indeed the Decade of Evangelism was "*In honour of Our Lady*". The cult of Mary is ever increasing whilst being nurtured in the bosom of the mother of cults.

The culmination of the Decade of Evangelism was to be a manifestation of the ecumenical super-church as the 'birds of a feather flocked together' under the leadership of the pope. It was the stated intention of the papacy to present Jesus Christ with a 2000th birthday present of a world more 'Christian' than not before a TV audience of an estimated 5 billion people on 25th December 2000. (The account of Satan's temptation of Christ in the wilderness (Luke 4:5-7) readily springs to mind at this point). This was to signal the commencement of the planned "Ecumenical Millennium" on 1 January 2001. Whilst many who were hoodwinked into this charade think that they were honouring the Lord Jesus they were in fact honouring the orchestrator of this Babel, Satan and his ambassador in this world, the Roman Antichrist, the Pope!

Herein lies the significance of the Ecumenical Movement of the 21st century: As Satan continues to build his new Babel using the brick of false religion and seeks to cement it together with the slime of a false spirit, biblical Christianity is being eroded and the glory that is due unto the one true and living God is being given to a Satanic counterfeit. The Satanic Super-church will arrive and it may be around for some time but we also know that as there ever has been a faithful remnant there ever shall be and our blessed Lord will destroy this Babel with the brightness of His coming. Even so come Lord Jesus.

CONCLUSION

Let us in conclusion turn again to the expert opinion of Dr Boettner for his comments upon Catholicism as a cult (sect):

"Another trait of the Roman Church is her attempt to brand all other church groups as 'sects,' and as schismatic. First, let us fix clearly in mind precisely what a 'sect' is. Dictionary definitions tend to emphasise the divisive, schismatic, heretical elements in defining a sect. Hence we would define a sect as a group that shuts itself in as Cod's exclusive people, and shuts all others out. By its exclusiveness a sect cuts itself off and isolates itself from the main stream of Christian life. On that basis the Roman Church, with its bigoted and offensive claim to be 'the only true church,' its readiness to brand all others as heretics, its anathemas, (or curses), so readily pronounced against all who dare to differ with its pronouncements, and its literally dozens of heresies and practices which are not found in the New Testament, automatically brands itself as the biggest and most prominent of all the sects."

Those religious groups who are commonly known as cults, understood to be by most people as cults, would vary in the marks of a cult that it may carry. Some would bear marks that others do not, yet they are clearly cults. Sadly some true churches bear some of the marks of cults at times and in some degree. Rome however bears all twelve marks of a cult, all of the time, in the fullest degree. Catholicism is the cult of all cults, and yet many, including good men like Walter Martin and Dave Breese don't seem to be able to see it! Perhaps they just don't want to see, but the evidence is nonetheless there for the entire world to see, and above all, God knows and will judge it accordingly in the final day. *"Wherefore come ye out from among them and be ye separate saith the Lord."*

How can any true Christian, one, whose life is guided by the Word of God, fellowship with a religious cult that is masquerading as Christianity? Looking at the mountain of evidence here before us, barely having touched upon the greater mountain of error that is Catholicism, we surely have enough to tell us that we should not countenance Catholicism in any shape or form. Ecumenism with Catholicism is an open betrayal of the Gospel of Jesus Christ.

THE NEED FOR RC EVANGELISM

So what now? It is not enough to declare Catholicism to be a cult and then just walk away with the attitude of 'I won that argument'. Winning arguments against Catholicism is very easy to do when one uses the searchlight of Holy Scripture to reveal its obvious flaws, just as simple as it is to destroy the tenets of any false cult or ism. The question is what do we do with the superior knowledge that we have? What superior knowledge? All that information on Catholicism about popes and confessionals and things? No! The superior knowledge that the Christian possesses is that the work of salvation is a finished work, a 'done' work! It must be shared with the lost in evangelism.

Romans chapter 10 is the great missionary chapter of the Bible it speaks of the need for believers to go forth preaching the good news of the Gospel to the religious but lost. It speaks of those who, not knowing the righteousness of God, go about to establish their own righteousness. It speaks of those who have not submitted themselves to Christ and His righteousness but rather rely on their works for salvation. It can be seen that this chapter in the book of Romans speaks of the need for Christians to evangelise, for Christians to evangelise Roman Catholic people.

But is it right to assert that there is a need for Christians to evangelise Catholics? There appear to be three basic objections as to why we shouldn't: I. Are they not already Christians, although of a different flavour? 2. Rome is changing isn't it? 3. Why bother at all? We shall be attempting to answer these objections as we go on with this study.

Sadly few Christians do bother attempting to evangelise Catholics and there are a number of reasons for this. For example: Apathy, a lack of knowledge of their own doctrine, a lack of understanding of Catholic doctrine, the influence of the Charismatic Movement, the current ecumenical scene etc.

If Roman Catholics believe the same as Christians then we would of course be wasting our time evangelising them. We would be 'preaching to the converted. If however they believe something different to that which Christians believe then they do need to be biblically evangelised. Before we go any further I think we should define just what we mean when we talk about Roman Catholics and Christians as it may vary quite a lot between what one Roman Catholic might believe and another does on any aspect of their religion. Also many Christians are often unclear as to what really qualifies as Christianity. Therefore we shall take the yardstick of both sides, their 'rule of faith', by which to measure them and compare them. The yardstick of

Catholicism being what the church teaches and the yardstick of the Christian being that which the Bible teaches. The Bible being the Word of God is without question the final authority.

By Roman Catholic we mean a person who adheres to the sacramental system of Roman Catholicism. A Roman Catholic is one who is trusting in the Roman Catholic system for salvation. A Christian is one who is fully and completely trusting in the Lord Jesus Christ for salvation. They are trusting in what Christ accomplished upon the cross of Calvary.

It would be fair to say that anyone, whether Roman Catholic, Hindu, Mormon, Jehovah's Witness, Moslem, Freemason, Buddhist or Jew, as they are all trusting in the finished work of Christ and following Him in obedience, they cannot be designated Christians. If however we have misunderstood Roman Catholicism and it does equate with what the Word of God teaches about the Christian faith, then we are redundant. Therefore let us take a look at some of the things which Christianity and Catholicism seem to have in common:

Some Comparisons: Roman Catholics say that they believe in Jesus: But is the Jesus of Catholicism the Jesus of the New Testament? Priest Despars is on record as having said in his homily one day 'Jesus did most of the work for our salvation. I would say about

157

90 percent. The poor Roman Catholic thinks this is wonderful news as it only leaves him or her with 10 percent to do. What they don't realise of course is that 10 percent of infinity is infinity. They could never complete this 10 percent and therefore salvation is not possible. The Roman Catholic Jesus is finite; he is limited in what he can do for them. By its very repetition the Mass proves its own worthlessness for it must continue on and on day in day out. Never completed. The finite Christ of Catholicism is tangible, can be carried to and fro, lifted up and set down. He can be crushed, he can corrupt, and a mouse could eat him. Why is this? For the finite Christ of Catholicism, when called from his throne in heaven in the Mass takes on the form of a small round wafer, and though this wafer is said to actually be Jesus Christ, in his fullness, and is offered as a sacrifice for the living and the dead, his being daily offered cannot complete the work for salvation!

What a contrast this is to the finished work of the Christ of the Bible. The Lord Jesus cried out from the cross "It is finished". The psalmist whilst writing of our Lord's passion in psalm 22 wrote. "He hath done".

In Hebrews chapter 10 we read "And every priest standeth daily ministering and offering oftentimes the same sacrifices which can never take away sins: (The Roman Catholic Mass). But this man. (Christ Jesus) after He had offered one sacrifice for sins forever, sat down on the right hand of God". Christ did a complete substitutionary work upon the cross of Calvary whilst the Catholic Jesus has been offered thousands of times daily in the sacrifice of the Mass yet the work is never completed. Priest Conway whilst writing in 'The Question Box' an Roman Catholic publication stated: "To assert that the guilt of man's sins was transferred to our Lord dying on the cross is absurd and blasphemous". This is in contradiction to what the Apostle Peter, whom this priest would have us believe was the first pope, said in his first letter for he wrote concerning Christ: "Who His own self bare our sins in His own body upon the tree" (2:24).

The doctrine of substitutionary atonement is a fundamental of the Christian faith and yet our Roman Catholic friends tell us that it is "absurd and blasphemous". Are they and we talking of the same Jesus? I believe not for the Christ of the Bible is the infinite Christ. "He is able also to save them to the uttermost that come unto God by Him".

We also find in the Bible that Jesus doesn't just point us to God and say 'well get on with it, do your best' but he actually brings us to God (1 Pt 3:18). Yet St Peter's Catechism states that *"It is the sin of presumption to believe that we can be saved by God alone without our own efforts".*

To recap then: The Roman Catholic Jesus is finite has not completed the work of salvation, did not bear the sins of many and does not bring sinners to God! This is not the Christ of the Bible for the Christ who poured out His life blood for me has done a perfect work of redemption and is bringing many sons unto glory among whom I count it a privilege to be numbered by the surety of God's Word. The Roman Catholic Jesus is sub scriptural and consequently any work of atonement must also be dubious worth or merit.

Some may say, 'OK maybe Roman Catholics have a few strange ideas about Jesus but they believe in the Holy Trinity, don't they?' Not exactly for there is a problem with the Roman Catholic trinity, it has four people in it!

A banner stretched across a Dublin street many years ago read "God Bless the Trinity". Now you may be forgiven for thinking that this is just Irish logic, and so would many if it wasn't for the fact that the Legion of Mary in 1958 were handing out tracts with the blasphemous text "Mary so loved the world that she gave her only begotten son". Incredible isn't it? But true.

In 1954 pope Pius XII said Mary is indeed worthy to receive honour and might and glory. She is exalted to hypostatic unity with the Blessed Trinity". That phrase 'hypostatic unity' is the same theological phrase that describes the unity between Father, Son and Holy Spirit. So again we find Roman Catholics using Christian terminology whilst meaning something else altogether. You may have a Roman Catholic friend that tells you that he or she is 'Born Again'. Before you flip a somersault and shout 'praise the Lord' just ask them when this was and how and no doubt you will receive an answer something like this:

'I was born again when I was baptised as a baby.' Being 'born again' for the Roman Catholic equates with infant baptism, as this is what their church teaches them. That they become Christians by being splashed with water. They don't of course, they merely become wet sinners instead of dry ones!

What does a Roman Catholic mean when they talk of being *'Saved by Grace?'* The Christian definition is that one is saved as a result of God's unmerited favour, without respect to our works. The Catholic however would say that God gives the ability to do the works necessary for salvation.

When your Roman Catholic friend says *'Jesus died for me'* he merely means that Jesus opened the gate to Heaven to make it possible for him to get to God. The Christian believer is able to say with confidence that

Jesus completed a substitutionary work on my behalf that brings me to God.

The Christian is *'justified by Faith'* which means that our right standing before God is due entirely to our trust in the completed work of Christ and God thereby regards us as judicially free. This is once again far removed from what the Roman Catholic means for he would say: 'By faith in the operation of the sacraments, we are brought to a position in which we are able to accomplish the works necessary for salvation.'

The believer knows that Heaven is a gift of God freely given but Catholicism says that *'not only does God give us Heaven as a free gift, He also gives us the added blessing of allowing us to pay for it'* Try this out on someone: buy then a nice gift and then tell them that they can have the added blessing of washing your dishes for the next six months to pay for it!

What does a Catholic mean when they say that they are saved? They mean that baptism and the Roman Catholic sacraments saved them. They are being saved by their taking advantage of the graces offered by their church. They hope to be saved when they stand before God in the last judgement. All this is far removed from what the Christian means by being saved for we would say: We were saved from the penalty of sin by the death of the Lord Jesus Christ for us. The indwelling Holy

Spirit is saving us from the power of sin. We will be saved from the very presence of sin when we go to Heaven.

What of assurance of salvation? The believer has assurance because he has a perfect Saviour but our Roman Catholic friends have no such assurance. They have only a *'hope so'* salvation which much of the time is based upon what they feel so they say things like 'God is doing many wonderful things in my life.' God is too loving to send anyone to Hell' and so forth. The Christian has a 'know so' salvation as opposed to the Roman Catholic's 'hope so' salvation. The believer is 'trusting Christ', relying upon His sacrifice as payment for sin. But the Roman Catholic says 'we trust him to help us to do whatever is necessary to get to Heaven'.

The terminology is the same but the meaning is totally different. The average Roman Catholic is not deliberately trying to deceive you, although there are those who will, but in the main most Roman Catholics are merely stating things as they understand them. As you can see from what we have been discussing there is a world of difference between Roman Catholicism and Christianity. Roman Catholicism is not Christianity; it may at first glance bear a resemblance but when we strip away the thin veneer we find what is in fact a counterfeit Christianity!

But Rome is changing isn't it? After all this pope seems so nice, so different to others.

This is a common objection to Christians evangelising Catholics and even if it were true surely it should inspire us to evangelise them all the more that we might bring them right around to a biblical point of view as speedily as possible. However, it isn't true, Rome has not changed one iota of its unbiblical dogma, nor can it, for to do so would be for it to admit that the infallible church had in fact erred. Its motto and boast is 'Semper Eadem'- Always the Same.'

Yes it is true that Rome now refers to Protestants as Separated Brethren" and that the Mass is now permitted in the vernacular, it is also true that some churches have altar girls instead of boys today. All this though is merely cosmetic, as the doctrine of Catholicism has in fact worsened as the years roll on. Catholicism can be likened to a woman who has had a hairdo, a manicure, her face made up and her best dress on. But she is still the same drunken prostitute no matter what finery you dress her in! At Vatican II all that had gone before in previous councils, the Pope and all the Bishops present reaffirmed, particularly the Council of Trent. All that was actually done was a lick of paint was applied to give an impression of newness.

This brings us to a further objection: *Why bother evangelising Catholics?*

The answer to this is quite simple - because there is a need. If you ask a doctor why he picks on sick people, he will tell you that there is a need. It is out of love for these lost men and women, boys and girls who are bound by religion and in obedience to our Lords command to witness for Him that we should seek to win souls for Christ. It ought to be as natural for a believer to witness of Christ as it is for dogs to bark. Lions roar, ducks quack, donkeys bray, Christians evangelise, and Christians should evangelise Catholics because there is a need. What then is the need of the Roman Catholic?

To discover this we must look at their condition and know the symptoms of their problem. The Bible likens the state of the lost to that of a blind man, someone in darkness. What then are they in need of? Light. *"The entrance of thy words giveth light"*. So we now know that our Catholic friends need God's Word. They don't need our humanistic reasoning, philosophical arguments or polemical assaults about wicked popes and such like but God's Word for it is the Bible which God has declared is *"the power of God unto salvation."*

Perhaps the thought has crossed your mind that Roman Catholics read the Bible nowadays and therefore they will be evangelised through this activity. This is a possibility, however, consider the Roman Catholic attitude towards bible study. Do they really study the Bible? The truth is that they may read a verse here and a verse there in private, and we should thank God that this is so, but within any organised teaching or study groups they are still only allowed to understand the Bible as the priest dictates. He in turn is only permitted to interpret the scriptures in accordance with the 'unanimous consent of the Church Fathers', and as one ex priest pointed out, the only thing that they were ever unanimous on was to disagree on just about everything.

Those who ignore the official line and do take the scriptures for themselves, asking for the guidance of the Holy Spirit, these are most often those that leave the Roman system of religion. For the entrance of God's word gives light!

There is a world of difference between Christianity and Roman Catholicism, or any other false religion for that matter. Christianity - Christ has done all the work for salvation. Catholicism and others - We must do part, or even all that is required for salvation. There is a need for Roman Catholics to be evangelised. To take the easy way out and ignore the spiritual need of your Catholic friend would be similar to a doctor deliberately ignoring the disease that is ravaging his patient. The best doctor is the doctor who recognises the need of his patient and is equipped to deal with him correctly. Likewise, the Christian who recognises the need of his Catholic friend to hear of the finished work of the Lord Jesus Christ is best qualified to administer the Gospel message.

To tell the truth is not bigotry or hatred. If you hated anyone you would leave him or her without the good news of the Gospel! A hateful man would not seek to bring sight to a blind man, light into a sin-darkened soul. Roman Catholics need the Gospel; they need you to tell them. You, friend, if you are truly a Christian, can lead Catholics to Christ!

We have already discussed the need for Roman Catholic evangelism. We asked the question 'Is there a need for Roman Catholic evangelism?' We have found that Roman Catholicism, whilst using Christian terminology, is in fact fatally sub-Christian.

We discussed the christ of Catholicism and found that he was finite, that he did not bear the sins of many, and that he does not bring sinners to God. We find that the Roman Catholic Jesus is only finite and consequently any work of atonement must also be and that this necessitates the continual offering in the sacrifice of the mass.

We have contrasted this finite christ of Roman Catholicism with the infinite Christ of the Bible "who by one offering hath perfected forever them that are sanctified'. (Heb 10: 14). The Lord Jesus Christ cried out from the cross 'It is finished' (Jn 19:30). The christ of Catholicism is still hanging upon the cross because he is still doing whilst the infinite Christ of the Bible has done, once and forever done.

We found that whilst Roman Catholics use Christian terminology they in fact they often mean the direct opposite. It is plain to see that whilst biblical salvation is all of grace, Roman Catholicism is all of works. We made the clear distinction between Christianity and Catholicism in this way: We said that: a Roman Catholic is one who is trusting in the Roman Catholic system of religion for salvation and that a Christian is one who is fully and completely trusting in the Lord Jesus Christ for salvation. It is quite apparent that Roman Catholicism is not the same thing as Christianity and that Roman Catholics do not believe the same things as Christians. The Roman Catholic is trusting in what he or she must *Do* whilst the Christian is trusting in what Christ has *Done*. We therefore concluded that there is indeed a need for Christians to evangelise Roman Catholics.

So let us now come to some aspects of Roman Catholic evangelism and consider: The Missionary, the

Missionfield, the Message, the Method and finally Mobilisation.

The Missionary: In Romans chapter 10 and the verse 14, 'How then shall they call on him in whom they have not believed and how shall they believe in him of whom they have not heard and how shall they hear without a preacher?" Preaching is not necessarily a formal discourse such as we find in our churches each Lord's day, indeed in the days of the early Church the spread of the Gospel was due more to Christians gossiping the Gospel to friends and relatives, neighbours and strangers. We can see examples of this in the Samaritan woman who, having met Christ, dashed off into the town to tell all she met about the Lord Jesus Christ. (Jn 4:28). Andrew, who having met Christ went first of all to his brother, Simon Peter with the good news that he had found the Messiah. (Jn 1:41). These were ordinary men and women who had no theological training, no tracts, and no bible. They were ordinary men and women like you and I. They gossiped the Gospel!

There are many that have the strange notion that witnessing for Christ is the job of the Pastor or someone designated as the outreach worker, or someone else. In fact anyone else, so long as it isn't them! The Bible teaches that evangelism is the responsibility and privilege of every believer .Personal evangelism and witness for Christ is expected: 'Ye have not chosen me, but I have chosen you, that ye should go and bring forth fruit', and that your fruit should remain:'(Jn 15:16). Personal evangelism is encouraged: 'And he (Jesus) saith unto them, Follow Me, and I will make you fishers of men. And they straightway left their nets and followed Him' (Mt 4:19-20). Personal evangelism is commanded: 'Go ye therefore, and teach all nations, baptising them in the same of the Father, and of the Son, and of the Holy Ghost: Teaching them to observe all things whatsoever I have commanded you:'(Mt 28:19-20). Personal evangelism is illustrated in many passages of scripture such as Jn 1:35-51, 3:1-16, 4:1-30 and Acts chapter 8.

There are many Christians who are not witnessing for Christ, as they should. Why is this? It could be that they have no vital experience of Christ to relate; they know their lives are inconsistent with what they want to profess; they have no concern for the lost or do not accept the Bible teaching as to their state without Christ. With many it is simply a fear of what others may think of them. Whatever their excuse it amounts to sin, the sin of unbelief, the sin of laziness or the sin of disobedience. If we are really following, we shall be fishing! If we are not fishing, are we following?

The first qualification of an effective evangelist is a personal assurance of salvation and satisfaction in Jesus

Christ. This will only come from a personal encounter and then a daily experience of Christ. This is to be found and cultivated through the Word of God and prayer. The second qualification is a working knowledge of the scriptures. Dr R.A. Torrey said: 'The effective soul winner should know his Bible so as to show a person his need of Christ, to show them that Christ is the saviour they need, to show them how to make this saviour their own personal Saviour and Lord.'

The Missionfield: In Romans 10 we read, verses 1-3, 'Brethren, my heart's desire and prayer to God for Israel is, that they might be saved. For I bear them record that they have a zeal of God, but not according to knowledge. For they being ignorant of God's righteousness, and going about to establish their own righteousness, have not submitted unto the righteousness of God.'

We read here of people who are zealous towards God but there is something they do not know. They are ignorant of God's righteousness, the imputed righteousness of the Lord Jesus Christ, and consequently go about to try and establish their own. These are a people that are doing. Roman Catholic people are quite often very zealous in their religion and because they do not know the perfect righteousness of Christ, because they do not know that the work of righteousness is finished, they are going about trying to

.

establish their own by their works.   Roman Catholic people are Doing people.

This is our missionfield, your missionfield. Mention the word missionary and immediately thoughts of far off lands, thousands of miles of travel, foreign languages and tribal peoples come to mind. Far too many Christians forget the missionfield on their own doorstep.

As we go about our daily business we come into contact with all sorts of people, many of whom are Roman Catholic. Whether they are Catholic or not doesn't really matter for if they are not trusting in the finished work of Christ they are lost, regardless of what label they may put on themselves. All the lost are Doing people for every false religion gives lots of things you must Do to attain salvation but we are primarily concerned today with our Roman Catholic friends, neighbours, relatives and others with which we come into contact.

Around your church and down your street, perhaps living right next door to you are Roman Catholic people. These are often good, honest, clean living, do anyone a good turn, very religious, kinds of people but the bottom line is that they are unsaved: Not because they have done good works, but because they have trusted good works, not because they have prayed, but because they have trusted prayer, not because they do not know someone whom they call christ, but because the christ they know is not the Christ of the Bible.

All this should be a great motivation to Catholic evangelism. If they all robbed banks we would still have an obligation to evangelise them, if they were all murdering thugs, which they are not, we would yet have an obligation to witness to them. But they don't, many Roman Catholics are dear, sweet, good-living people. The underlying tragedy of their lives is that, filled with thoughts of religion, praying, meriting, working, they are ignorant of the righteousness of God.

The Message: You have perhaps noticed that the words *Do* and *Done* keep cropping up. The reason for this is that these words are an absolute contrast and show the difference between works and grace. If we were to use the words, black and white, how black is black or how white is white. There is room for various shades of grey in between and it is therefore not a good contrast. However with Do and Done we know that you can only Do a job until it is Done.

Our Catholic friends need to know that they cannot be doing and done at the same time. If Christ has done then there is nothing that they can do to add to that. To say that there is anything more to be done is to say that Christ did an imperfect work of salvation and to say this is to malign His person. What our doing Catholic friends need to hear then is that the work for salvation is Done. In Romans 10:4 we read 'For Christ is the end of the law for righteousness to everyone that believeth'. Christ has Done that which they cannot do for themselves, he has paid the penalty of sin in full. Roman Catholic people need to know that:

Man has offended a Holy God because of their sin. (Rom 3:23). 'For all have sinned and come short of the glory of God'.

That God has lovingly offered pardon and redemption through the perfect sacrifice of His Son. (Rom 5:8) 'But God commendeth His love towards us, in that while we were yet sinners, Christ died for us.'

That whoever puts their trust in God's provision will be eternally saved. (Jn 3:16). 'For God so loved the world that He gave His only begotten Son that whosoever believeth in Him should not perish but have everlasting life'.

That nothing they have done, are doing or hope to do will ever save them. (Isaiah 64:6). 'All our righteousnesses are as filthy rags'.

They need to know that: 'Christ is the end of the law for righteousness to everyone that believeth'.

The Method: There is no magic formula for winning Roman Catholics to Christ but there are two basic methods, Rote Evangelism and Response Evangelism. There are some that advocate the use of methods such as the Romans Road and if interrupted by a question they say, "I'll come back to that". They rarely do of course and the person being evangelised concludes that they were not interested in what he had to say but merely in finishing their presentation. This is Rote Evangelism, a kind of evangelistic recipe or recitation, which once performed on an unsaved person's doorstep hopefully results in a decision for Christ. The mind-set of the evangelist (so called) is that nothing must get in the way of this recipe for heaven, he must get this scalp, and put another tick in on his score card.

How rude can one be? Here we are on someone's doorstep and we have basically just told him or her that we don't care about what he has to say to us and that what we have to say is much more important. This kind of evangelism is contrived as well as being rude and results in decisional regeneration, which is not regeneration at all.

In Response Evangelism you are seeking to start a conversation about spiritual things but you want to include the person whom you are seeking to evangelise in your conversation. You are interested in what he or she has to say and you respond to it with biblical truth.

If you use a presentation such as the Romans Road to start your conversation don't be bound by it, don't be afraid to depart from it. If someone asks a question of you during your presentation, answer it. If you don't know the answer, say so and tell them that you will find out and come back to them, making sure that you do. Often the greatest difficulty, is starting a conversation that is going to lead us to the point we want to get to, - the finished work of the Lord Jesus Christ.

A good opener might be to ask 'between now and the day that you die, is there anything you must DO to be sure of Heaven?'. No doubt you will be given any number of things that they feel they must DO as there are literally thousands of things that Catholicism gives them to DO. You then have a perfect opportunity to share with them the finished work of the Lord Jesus Christ.

The testimony method can be useful. Ask what their hopes of heaven are and you will get many different answers, the one answer you probably won't get is the biblical one if they are Roman Catholic. They will say things like 'I've lived a good life', 'I hope to get there some day through the sacraments and purgatory'. After they have told you of their hope so salvation tell them of your know so salvation because of the perfect work of the Lord Jesus Christ and the surety of God's Word.

Another good opening might be to ask 'Do you have a Bible?' Many Roman Catholics do these days, they might dash off to find it and proudly bring it to you whilst blowing off the dust. It may well turn out to be a Missal or a prayer book, but it is all very much the same thing to our Catholic friend.

Don't ask what version, that is a side issue, but do ask them 'do you read it?' They may say yes whilst meaning that perhaps once or twice a year they might read a verse or two. Tell them that you are genuinely glad that they do read it. Then you might say something like: 'The Blessed and Holy Apostle Saint John wrote five books of the Bible. In chapter 5 of his first letter he, wrote these words: "These things are written unto you that believe on the name of the Son of God that ye may know that ye have eternal life" Ask 'do you believe on the name of the Son of God?' Draw your listener to answer. Show him from the Bible that he can *know* whether he has eternal life. Emphasise the present knowledge of salvation and explain that eternal life is a life that lasts forever and ever. The aim is to get into conversation about spiritual things with them without getting the door slammed in your face. It is not easy. Each time they come at you with a DO counter it with the DONE of the Gospel.

Here are ten basic rules for Roman Catholic evangelism as given by the late Dr Bill Jackson of 'Christians

Evangelising Catholics', slightly edited by myself, which will reinforce much of what has already been said.

1. *Your primary motive must not be to get results.* Whilst there is nothing wrong with getting results if we make it our primary motive we will make our Gospel presentation as shallow as it has to be in order to get the persons response. Neither is it good to have a burden for souls as our primary motive. We should be concerned for the lost but the only acceptable primary motive is that we want to glorify God. This primary motivation will enable us to be Christ-like witnesses. Remember God requires that we be 'faithful', not successful servants.

2. *Don't be in a hurry.* Be Patient. Bart Brewer, an ex-priest, has said: "No farmer, ploughs, sows and reaps in twenty minutes." Because the mind of a Roman Catholic has been conditioned differently, he will not even understand many of the things that you say to him. We often have to build relationships to effectively evangelise. This does not mean a person cannot get saved in twenty minutes, but if it takes longer, be willing to spend time in the scriptures; don't become obnoxious, but lovingly and persistently explain God's plan of salvation. Don't give up.

3. *Never assume that your Catholic friend understands you even if he agrees with you.* He recognises that you seem to know a lot about the Bible, and, rather than admit that he doesn't know something that would give you an opportunity to prove him wrong from the Bible, he might agree with everything you say. Also many Catholics are taught to use biblical terminology and may seem to agree with you. But remember, they have our vocabulary, but not our dictionary.

4. *Try to keep from arguing.* You must be willing to defend your faith biblically, and give a reason, for the hope that is within you, but an argument is seldom profitable. Some Christians seem to think that Jesus said 'Go into all the world and win arguments with every creature.' If you win an argument, you merely demonstrate how smart you are; if you preach the Gospel, you are telling them how perfect Christ is.

5. *Don't knock their church.* Some think that the greatest evangelistic weapon is to tell of tunnels between convents and monasteries and the bones of babies found there. A Priest would probably think it an absurd accusation as he might ask "Why would we bother to dig tunnels when we can just walk into a convent at any time'?"

Some Christians are shocked by the immorality of some priests and can't wait to air their thoughts but when you have a group of unregenerate men living in abnormal circumstances it shouldn't surprise us when they fall into sin.

6. *Be loving.* Catholics are not lost because they are awful people. As has been said earlier, many are sweet, devout and sincere people. Think of the tragedy of a mind being conditioned in youth, and because of this, being a slave to a Satanic religious system. Make Paul's prayer your prayer, "My heart's desire ... is that they might be saved'. Don't go with a superior attitude, but ask God to give you a love for them that only he can give you.

7. *Be biblical.* Some profound logic or devastating argument that your mind has produced will accomplish nothing in true evangelism. The Lord Jesus appointed one administrator of salvation, the Holy Spirit. It is He who convicts, reveals Jesus and baptises into His body. The Sword of the Spirit is the Word of God. If you give a testimony or use an illustration, make sure it is based upon biblical truth. The Bible is powerful. It is the entrance of God's Word that giveth light.

8. *Don't give him something to do.* Without realising their mistake, many people on visitation are trained to: a. get the person to repeat a prayer, b. get him to walk the aisle on Sunday, and c. get him to be baptised. The Catholic person is already thinking DO and he may

well have a go at doing those things if he thinks it will give him a better shot at Heaven. Don't give him something to DO for while he is thinking DO he is not trusting the 'DONE of the finished work of Christ.

9. *Answer his questions.* Never tell a sinner that you will answer his question later, as you may be missing the greatest opportunity to present the Gospel along a line in which he has already shown interest. Unless of course you are genuinely stuck for an answer Here you can perhaps say 'I don't know, I'll come back to you on that'. Thus making a second opportunity to speak.

10. *Don't dwell on non-essentials.* We can argue that Catholics worship Mary but we would certainly be better asking our Roman Catholic friend if Mary is a mediator, and then point out that a mediator always makes peace between warring parties. Use Romans 5:1 to tell of the true reconciliation with God. 'Therefore being justified by faith we have peace with God through our Lord Jesus Christ.'

Mobilisation. We have considered: The missionary, the missionfield, the message and the method. We are now ready for mobilisation. If you have decided to witness to Roman Catholics don't wait for others to catch the bug too, you could be waiting a long time. When going door to door, go in twos at least. One of you can pray silently whilst the other is speaking. Pray before you set out. Get others to pray for you whilst you are out.

Never interrupt your partner or correct them whilst they are speaking. Only interject if they seem to be stuck. Don't take a large Bible. You may frighten some people off. Use a pocket Bible or a New Testament. Do take a selection of suitable tracts. Do brush your teeth. Don't announce where you are from straight away. Wait until they ask. Just tell them initially that you are from a local church, (as all evangelism should be local church based). Don't worry if you make a mess of it. Try to learn from your mistakes and keep on trying.

What if they get mad? Many shun witnessing to Catholics because they sometimes get mad and we are often afraid of offending people and losing friendships. If you are a friend to a Roman Catholic, the proof of real friendship is caring. Do you care where your friend will spend eternity? Few Catholics get saved without getting mad first, for this is a natural reaction when they are challenged. Be sure you are loving in your approach, and then positively evangelise Roman Catholics.

Christians who are in the business of evangelising Roman Catholics are DONE people, going to DO people, using the Word of God to show that the work of salvation is DONE.

Every false religionist in this world is in some way or another trying to earn heaven, or their idea of redemption. Catholicism is likewise a system of works geared to giving its adherents lots of things to do to earn salvation. What Roman Catholics need is not for someone to go and tell them how bad their religion is, but just how wonderful the Christ of the Bible is and of the wonderful perfect work that he has completed, finished, done! Christians are, says Bill Jackson of Christians Evangelising Catholics, 'DONE people, going to 'DO' people, telling them that the work for salvation is indeed 'DONE'.

May God bless you as you seek to win those benighted souls in the darkness of the Roman cult of Antichrist for Christ. Amen.

God is Good Ministry

Email: goodenough4heaven@gmail.com

SOURCES

Title	*Author*	*Publisher*
The Vatican Bank	Bill Jackson	
The History of Protestantism Vols 1 & 2	JA Wylie	Mourne Missionary Trust
Ecclesiastical History	JL Von Moshiem	Howell
The Catholic Church Against the 20th Century	Avro Manhattan	Watt's & Co
The Two Babylons	Alexander Hislop	Loizeux Bros
Book of Martyrs	J Foxe	Secker/Warburg
Treatise on Relics	J Calvin	Johnstone/Hunter
Roman Catholicism	L Boettner	Pres & Reformed Pub Co
Catholicism Analysed	J McDonald	Scottish Reformation Soc
Freedom's Foe	A Pigott	Wickliffe Press
Awful Disclosures of	Maria Monk	
Rise and Fall of the Roman Catholic Church	F P Peterson	
Paganry, Popery, Pillage	C Labarum	Thynne/Jarvis Ltd
An Exposure of Popery	W Anderson	Hodder/Stoughton
Delineation of Catholicism	C Elliot	Weslyen Conference
Catholicism and Truth Vols 1 & 2	GG Coulton	Faith Press
Roman Catholicism	CH Wright	Religious Tract Society
Fifty Years in the Church of Rome	C Chiniquy	Chick
Noble Army of Heretics	Bill Jackson	Colonial Baptist Press
Christians Guide to Roman Catholicism	Bill Jackson	Colonial Baptist Press

Catholic Terror Today	Avro Manhattan	Paravision Pubs
Secrets of Catholicism	J Zachello	Loizeux Bros
Vatican Finances	C Pallenburg	Penguin
The World's Religions	N Smart	Cambridge Uni Press
Book of Mormon	J Smith	CoJCoLDS
New World Translation of the Holy Scriptures		Watchtower
Know the Marks of Cults	Dave Breese	Victor Books
Cults - The Battle For God	S Harrison	Helm
Kingdom of the Cults	W Martin	Bethany House
Adventures in Reconciliation	P Monaghan	Eagle
Meetings with Mary	JT Connell	Virgin Publishing
The Teaching of the Catholic Church	K Rahner	Mercier Press
This is the Faith	Canon Ripley	Fowler/Wright
Dictionary of Moral Theology	Cardinal Roberti	Burns/Oates
Catholic Dictionary	Addis/Arnold	Virtue & Co
The Church Visible	JC Noonan	Penguin
Catholicism Vol 1 & 2	RP McBrien	Chapman
Pastoral Companion	MJ Mathis	Ecclesia Press
Concise Theological Dictionary	K Rahner	Burns/Oates
Catechism of the Catholic Church		Chapman
Documents of Vatican II	WM Abbott	Chapman
Vatican Council II	A Flannery	Dominican Pubs
A Catechism of Christian Doctrine		Catholic Truth Society

186

Made in the USA
Monee, IL
05 August 2023

40483729R00105